Enjoy Cooking!
Enjoy Entertaining!
Enjoy the Experience!
=

Elizabeth Hurst Stone

An Invitation to Entertain

Recipes for Gracious Parties

bright sky press

HOUSTON, TEXAS

2365 Rice Blvd., Suite 202
Houston, Texas 77005

10   9   8   7   6   5   4   3   2

Library of Congress Cataloging-in-Publication Data

Stone, Elizabeth, 1962-
An invitation to entertain : recipes for gracious parties / by Elizabeth Stone ; photography by Michael Hart ;
event design by Cynthia Stone.
p. cm.
ISBN 978-1-936474-21-9 (hardback)
1. Entertaining. 2. Menus. I. Title.

TX731.S737 2012
642'.4--dc23   2012004509

Editorial Direction, Lucy Herring Chambers
Creative Direction, Ellen Peeples Cregan
Design, Marla Y. Garcia

Photo credits: Stephanie Harding, pages 47 & 49; Larry Fagala, pages 57-59, 105-110 & 225.
All other photography, Michael Hart; Event Design, Cynthia Stone
Printed in Canada through Friesens

An Invitation to Entertain

Recipes for Gracious Parties

Elizabeth Stone

Photography by Michael Hart   Event Design by Cynthia Stone

bright sky press

HOUSTON, TEXAS

Dedication

*To my mother, for giving me the gift of hospitality,
sharing her passionate love of people and teaching me perseverance;
To my father, for always pushing me to reach for higher
levels and teaching me to never give up;
To my wonderful family, friends and employees—past and present—
for loving me, standing by me through thick and thin,
and teaching me more than I could have imagined;
And, as always, to the Glory of God,
for his endless and unconditional Grace;
with Him all things are possible.*

Entertaining

Parties & Particulars

a Memorable Event

F ood, cooking and entertaining are as much about the experience as they are about creating and eating wonderful food. The taste and quality of your food are—of course—important, but the experience is what your guests remember most.

Have you ever eaten at a restaurant with an exceptional waiter and a so-so meal? You remember what a great evening it was, and you'll probably go there again because you enjoyed yourself. But, the alternative is not true. When the fabulous meal is destroyed by the surly and insulting waiter, I don't know about you, but I never go back to those restaurants. All I remember is the bad taste left in my mouth from the service.

A memorable event begins with a warm, inviting environment. My mother would always say to our arriving guests, "Come in this house!" Although it reads like a command, she said it in such a loving way that guests felt they were being welcomed into their own home. She used her special plates, put fresh flowers around our home and made every guest feel like the guest of honor. In every event I'm involved in today, I try to recreate the sense of easy and gracious hospitality that

was such a defining part of her.

My mother made everyone feel appreciated, especially me. I love to reflect on all the fun experiences and parties that she created for me from the time I was a very little girl. In 1962, my mother was forty-five and my father, fifty. They had done "the baby thing:" my sister was fifteen and my brother ten. My birth was quite a surprise, but I was immediately welcomed into our family and included in my mother's entertaining.

By the time I was three years old, eating out, attending parties and using good manners were everyday experiences. I learned to socialize with friends of all ages, and my palette was most sophisticated. By the age of five I was already eating asparagus, artichokes, duck and lamb—quite unusual foods for a child to eat back then.

The door was always open at our house. Family and friends stopped by for dinner often. The gift of making others feel special was an art form perfected by my mother. When you came to our house—whether my friend or hers, whether invited or not—you were always welcome and always offered food and beverage—vodka soda with a lemon twist? How about a spicy Bloody Mary? Or—on a hot afternoon—would you care for an icy TaB? She almost always kept cheese cookies and Texas Trash on hand, and pimento cheese was kept stocked in the fridge.

From my nursery school days, Mom invited my friends into our home. She sat and visited with us, day in and day out, sharing juice and cookies. My friends quickly became fond of her. They felt her love and kindness, and we all enjoyed each other's company. I didn't realize it then, but my mother was teaching me the art of entertaining: You invite people in, offer them something to eat and drink and make them feel special. It's very simple.

Gracious hospitality is one of the greatest gifts that you can give your family and friends. I've spent two decades catering parties and events of all sizes. At the heart of each, is my mother's simple formula. Now, I've collected my favorite recipes and entertaining ideas so you can use them to entertain with confidence and joy. Whether you're an experienced event planner or a first-time fearful party giver, you can use the proven power of breaking bread in a way that tantalizes the senses and creates experiences that warm the hearts of others.

Entertaining should be fun. It's not necessary to spend lots of money or go over the top on food or décor to have a great party. If you love to cook, then do so. If you love food, then make it a central part of the event. If not, hire a caterer or get the food from a restaurant or specialty store. If you're hosting a large affair, hire an event planner. The most important thing is to do what makes you feel comfortable so you can be a cheerful and warm host or hostess. If you focus on providing gracious hospitality first, your events will be memorable, and you'll have fun, too.

Let's get this party started!

ELIZABETH STONE AN INVITATION TO ENTERTAIN

Daytime Delights

When I think of the early part of the day,

I think energy, brightness and fun. Daytime events provide a great venue for entertaining. You can hold them indoors or out, and you have the option of offering lighter and often less expensive foods and beverages. They provide a festive change from the usual routine, and daylight is so happy. Natural lighting is without question my favorite—it adds a special warmth and ambiance to a party. Use your creativity and bring the brightness of the morning into your event.

M E N U

Cheese Cookies

Smoked Salmon Roulades
Ribbons of Smoked Salmon rolled around Chive and Lemon Zest Cream Cheese
with Red Onions and Capers,
served on a Toast Round and garnished with Fresh Dill

Spring Greens Salad
with Raspberries, Blueberries, Bleu Cheese,
Toasted Pecans and Raspberry Vinaigrette

Eggs Benedict Crepes
delicately Scrambled Eggs with finely diced Ham
rolled in a White Crepe, finished with a Hollandaise Sauce and Chives

Chicken Crêpes Provence
delicate homemade Crêpes filled with Roasted Diced Chicken Breasts
and Sautéed Mushrooms, finished with a Sherry Cream Sauce

Toasted Blueberry Muffins
with Honey Butter Glaze

Mandarin Orange Mousse
garnished with Mandarin Oranges with fresh Mint

Tartlets
Raspberry
Lemon Curd with Whipped Cream and Lemon Zest
Key Lime with Whipped Cream and Lime Zest
Dark Chocolate Grenache with Shaved Chocolate

Brandy Milk Punch

CHAMPAGNE BRUNCH

One of my favorite gifts to offer a wedding couple is a brunch on the day of the wedding. The bride and groom have so many tasks to conquer, and having their guests entertained while they get ready for the ceremony lifts a huge burden from their shoulders. A start and finish time on the invitation notifies guests that they may come and go as desired.

Weddings have no more real challenges than any event that we cater. But when you add the high emotions of the day to the normal controlled chaos of entertaining, things can get a little crazy. Both as hostesses and professional caterers we can sometimes get caught up in trying to take care of everything ourselves, and create more turmoil than necessary.

Once when catering a seated dinner wedding recep-

tion for 150 guests, I became the chaos creator. Should I know better? Yes. But sometimes I just can't help myself.

The main entrée for the dinner was beef tenderloin filets. Usually, this is my favorite. It's easy to do for a lot of guests, and if you over-cook beef tenderloin filets, they're still tender. More often than not at events like this, we're preparing food in spaces that are not really kitchens. To keep the beef heated, we use a catering item called a hot box. At this wedding, the first thing I did was put too much gel fuel in the hot box. It caught on fire. It was not a pretty sight. After whisking the box outside, I needed to come up with a new plan to cook

the filets, immediately. In my brilliance, I decided to cook all 150 steaks on the plating line using a camping butane burner and a skillet.

Not a good idea. When plating dinners, I like to be at the end of the line, garnishing, saucing and wiping the plates, and then double checking each plate as it goes out. It was impossible for me to cook the steaks and do all that. I created the problem, and I was the problem. Finally, one of my cohorts stepped in to save me. "Liz, maybe you should let someone else cook the steaks so that we can keep the line going." The food and the party were saved, no thanks to me.

I learned that I don't have to take on everything. It's

ok to delegate event tasks. True success in entertaining doesn't come from doing it all by myself, or even in not making mistakes. Success is how we handle and manage the inevitable mistakes. Do your best, and allow yourself to accept the gift of not being perfect. Put a smile on your face and realize that most things will never be noticed by anyone but you.

The brunch pictured here was a wedding shower. It took place in our client's rustic summer cottage garden.

Since much of her garden had already bloomed, our challenge was to bring it back to life. Hot pink tablecloths and a colorful "table" garden created the look of a full-blooming garden. I always try to include my client's personal items in the décor. In this case, the hostess was an artist, so we used some of her artwork to adorn the tables. I love the festive look of this event and all the bright colors!

HOW TO CREATE A TABLE GARDEN

My sister and I love to collaborate on creative projects. When she envisioned a table garden and told me to create it, I was—as usual—up for the challenge. I started with OASIS® cages, (floral foam in plastic cages which are available at floral supply and craft stores.) I lined them up next to each other. After soaking the OASIS®, I started with the larger flowers and then filled in with smaller ones. This type of arrangement makes a huge impact. It looks elaborate and expensive, but all it takes is a little time and creativity.

FLOWER ARRANGING

Flowers are an important part of every event, but they take on extra significance at weddings. Arranging your own flowers is a great way to lessen the burden on your pocketbook. Buying flowers in season is much less expensive than buying the same flower when it is out of season. Spring brings all of my favorites: peonies, lilies, delphinium, viburnum, hydrangea, and roses.

Look in your own garden for plant material you can use in your arrangement. You'll be surprised by how much you might find: aspidistra, magnolia leaves, long grasses, stones, gravel and herbs, just for starters. And that neighbor with the beautiful forsythia? It might just be time to get to know her a little better.

When selecting flowers, consider the colors that you want to highlight. Choose three to five colors for an arrangement, unless you want to create a monochromatic piece. You'll want a variety of textures and sizes as well. You can use very small "filler" flowers or seasonal greenery to soften the arrangement. Select flowers that are not completely open yet. Wherever you purchase your flowers, be sure to get the little packets of flower food to increase the longevity of your arrangement.

When you arrive home with your flowers, give the stems a fresh cut. Floral clippers are best, but you may also use sharp scissors or a sharp knife. Make sharp clean cuts. If the stems get crushed, it stresses the flowers and prevents them from absorbing water. Put the cut stems in a bucket of water with the flower food packet in it. Try to arrange your flowers on the day of the event so you'll know just how each bloom will look. If you need to arrange the flowers ahead of time, store them in a cool room overnight, and keep a few extras in the bucket to replace blooms that don't make it overnight.

When you're ready to arrange your flowers, plan the arrangement before you begin cutting stems. You can group flowers together to get maximum color impact, or create a more traditional style by equally dispersing the various flowers to create balance in the arrangement. There are many types of containers that you can use. Look around your house for pretty bowls, pitchers or tureens that would hold flowers. Whatever type of container you use, you'll need to stabilize your flower stems. If you're using a silver bowl, put pre-soaked OASIS® in it (see side bar). For other containers you can use a wire mesh to create a grid across the rim of the bowl with floral tape, or fill the container with curly willow or other pliable branches. If you're using a glass vase, make sure and use mechanics that are aesthetically pleasing or hide them with large leaves.

Have fun as you work with the blooms, and remember that you're creating an arrangement of beautiful flowers, not an entry in a flower show. There are no rules to follow except your own. Use the bride's favorite flower; use your grandmother's Blue Willow bowl; use an old silver ice bucket or a new glass cylinder. There are more wonderful ways to arrange flowers than any of us can begin to imagine. With fresh flowers and a lovely container, it's hard to go wrong and easy to make your table or sideboard festive.

**M
E
N
U**

Sweet and Spicy Almonds and Pecans

Champagne Brie Soup
in a demitasse cup

Citrus Salad
Grapefruit and Orange Salad with Avocado and Bacon
with Mom's vinaigrette

English Shrimp Curry
Curry Sauce with Sauteed Shrimp
White Rice

Condiments:
Toasted Slivered Almonds
Toasted Coconut
Mango Chutney
Golden Raisins
Riced Eggs
Orange Zest
Candied Ginger
Green Onions
Crumbled Bacon

Yeast Rolls

Lace Cookies

Old Fashioned Butter Toffee with Almonds

Chocolate Truffles

Vodka Gimlets, Ice Cold
served in silver goblets with Candied Lime slices

Winter

LADIES LUNCH

This luncheon is a tribute to my mother and her dear friends. These ladies gathered weekly for as long as I can remember to play Mahjong, a game that seems to me a cross between dominos and bridge. Every year during December, instead of playing, they shared a special lunch to celebrate the holiday season. The menu here is the exact menu that my mother served at this gathering every year, over at least twenty years. I love this meal, and whenever it was time for it, I would always get excited. I am so happy to be able to share it with you now.

23

COLLECTIONS AS DECORATION

Here is my personal collection of paperweights. When I was eight years old, my mother took me to an antique auction. I was so curious with the whole process I convinced her to find me something to bid on. The only small item in the whole building was a paperweight, which I successfully captured with a twelve-dollar bid. Little did I know that purchasing this paperweight would lead me to love and collect these glass jewels. Paperweights date back to the mid-nineteenth century in France. Ranging in size from about one to four inches, they hold beautiful pieces of artwork under a dome of glass. What do you have that is beautiful and might enhance your table?

MAHJONG

Dating back over two thousand years, Mahjong is said to have originated in the court of the King of Wu. Within this court, a great beauty lived in seclusion. To keep herself from utter boredom, she carved domino-shaped pieces of ivory and bamboo and created this unusual game. If a mental challenge is what you are looking for, mahjong is definitely your game. It was often called the "game of a hundred intelligences" simply because it required much concentration.

Afternoon Affairs

Lazy afternoons are such a luxury in our busy world, it's important to schedule them. When we send out an invitation for an afternoon event, and look forward to it, it becomes an invitation to relax together with friends and family. As the sun makes its way across the sky, a tea party can be just the thing to revive our spirits and put all agendas except enjoyment aside. Opportunities for teas are plentiful—graduations, weddings, birthdays, new babies, introducing new friends to old and just celebrating each other.

Tea has an interesting history. While tea itself was introduced into Britain in the 1600s, the ritual we recognize as a tea party was not common until the late 1700s. Before that time, the English dined twice a day: once in the morning and then in the evening. The latter meal, called dinner, was long and drawn-out, very late in the day.

Anna, the Duchess of Bedford (1788-1861), was prone to sinking spells around four in the afternoon. One summer day, the Duchess asked her servants to bring her a pot of tea and some bread. She began inviting her friends to join her for "tea" at Belvoir Castle. When her friends came, she asked the servants to prepare little sweet cakes, butter and sugar sandwiches and delicate sweets.

When the Duchess returned to London that fall, she continued having these gatherings. She invited her friends to come for tea and a walk during the afternoon. Other society hostesses quickly adapted the practice, and the afternoon tea began.

MENU

Red Wine Poached Pear on Brie Croustade

Homemade Apple Cinnamon Raisin Pecan Rolls

Ooey Gooey Orange Rolls

Dried Cherry, Cranberry and Currant Scones
with Clotted Cream

Ribbons of Smoked Salmon
with Curried Egg Salad
on an Endive Leaf

Banana, Fig and Walnut Bread Sandwiches
with Cream Cheese

Fresh Fruit Skewers
with Poppy Seed Dressing

Tarragon Chicken Salad
in Pastry Cups

Zucchini Bread

Strawberries and Grapes with Crème Fraiche and Powdered Sugar

Assorted Hot Teas
with Condiments

Cooking up a Celebration
WITH CHILDREN

After many fun experiences in the kitchen with my niece, Miss Serena, she and I decided that we needed to share with her friends. Here is what you need to know about Serena: she is ten, she *loves* anything pink, and she adores afternoon tea.

Together, we created an event for her and seven of her friends. They arrived after school and participated in making the sandwiches and cookies. Then they sat down to a formal—or not so formal, actually— English Tea. What fun we all had! The girls loved dipping the strawberries in chocolate, assembling the cookies and making the sandwiches. They felt as if they had planned the entire event.

I love to work with kids in the kitchen. They have no fears and no preconceived notions of how things are supposed to be. Basically, anything goes. All they

want is to have fun and create something good to eat. Whenever I spend time in the kitchen with children, I come away thinking that all cooking should be like this. Fun, fun, fun is the name of the game.

When I plan a children's event, I try to select food items that both the children and the adults will enjoy. Often, a client wants two different menus. I always suggest that it would be doing them a favor to introduce new and fun foods beyond the omnipresent chicken tender.

For Serena's event, the girls and I had a wonderful kitchen for the preparation of the food. If you don't have the room or the desire to have flour and powdered sugar everywhere, set up tables with butcher paper on

the driveway. Put all the ingredients out on the tables, and give the children instruction and let them have fun. It's amazing to watch their satisfaction as they get to eat food they actually made.

After the cookies, strawberries and sandwiches were made, we all sat down to a lovely afternoon tea with real china and silver. Children love to be pampered just as much as grown-ups do. They were so pleased with themselves, and—believe it or not—they all had wonderful manners. A few of the girls had about eight big chocolate covered strawberries, but what's life without a little extra chocolate?

For a more casual event, you can make or purchase

sugar cookie dough. Place piles of flour on the butcher paper and cut pieces of cookie dough. Have a variety of sprinkles, chocolate chips and icing to use for decorating. Small aprons and paper chef's hats are good and useful favors. Guests can roll the dough or hand pat the cookies to shape them. The flour will keep the dough from sticking and will also give them a little something to throw at each other. Messy is fun, and

great for photos.

Once the guests are finished decorating, send them off to swim or play in the sprinkler. While they are busy, bake the cookies. They'll be hot and delicious and ready for the kids to devour when they've dried off. A cookie decorating party is a simple event, but it's a guaranteed crowd pleaser.

Let the flour fly!

KEEPING FINGER SANDWICHES FRESH

I've had a lot of success over the years with finger sandwiches. Although, I think of finger sandwiches as a very simple item, people are always commenting that they find mine particularly good. After much thought and observation over the years, these are the reasons I've concluded our sandwiches are so appreciated. Use these tricks and yours will be, too.

- *Always use very fresh bread.*

- *Finger sandwiches dry out very easily—use lots of mayonnaise, butter or cream cheese on your sandwiches. This spread keeps the moisture in the sandwiches and keeps the filling from soaking into the bread and making the sandwich dry. I call this a fat barrier.*

- *Most importantly, place damp (not wet) paper towels on both sides of the sandwiches and store them in the refrigerator until just before serving. If you tray the sandwiches for an event, place them on the tray and cover them with damp paper towels until just before serving.*

- *If you make your sandwiches ahead of time, the night before for example, package as stated above and wrap very securely with plastic wrap. This keeps the moisture in and keeps them very fresh.*

TOP KID-FRIENDLY GADGETS

- ***The George Foreman Grill:*** *Most of us have one of these classics in the pantry somewhere. Get it out again, and older children can assemble and press hot sandwiches for a quick weeknight family meal while you tackle the sides.*

- ***A Plastic Knife:*** *For young children between the ages of three and seven, parents should get a plastic knife. Kids can learn how to handle the tool while doing prep work for you, including slicing soft foods like boiled potatoes, chicken breasts, tomatoes, avocados, green peppers and greens.*

- ***A Colorful Spoon:*** *When kids have their own set of utensils—spoons, spatulas, a cutting board—they'll be more likely to use them. Opt for something colorful. Try starting with one tool, and then add another over time.*

- ***Scissors:*** *Capable home cooks use kitchen shears to snip fresh herbs or green onions, and kids of all ages can do the same thing.*

- ***Vegetable and Garlic Choppers:*** *Super-safe, plastic-enclosed vegetable dicers with handles are available at specialty kitchen stores.*

- ***Vegetable Peelers:*** *By age four, kids can use vegetable peelers to peel carrots or make zucchini ribbons. Just give them the straight traditional kind, and remember to show them how to peel away from themselves.*

- ***Measuring Cups and Spoons:*** *Helping with measurements is a perfect task for any child old enough to grip a cup.*

- ***Pasta Machine:*** *Kids as young as three can use a pasta machine to roll and cut their own spaghetti.*

TIPS FOR COOKING WITH KIDS

Kids love to help cook. It makes them feel a part of the process, and it's an important way for them to learn skills. Here are some things I've learned from working with kids in the kitchen:

1. **Feed their interest.** When your kids show interest in something you are doing in the kitchen, involve them—let them stir batter or break the eggs.

2. **Set them up to feel accomplished.** None of us like the feeling of someone hovering, waiting to point out what's wrong. Unless they're in danger of completely ruining the meal, let them measure a little less than perfectly, grease the pan somewhat incompletely, and stir a bit too much.

3. **Give recipes or meals a theme.** Use holiday themed candies and icing, like candy corn for Halloween and candy hearts for Valentine's Day. Use themes of activities they like: sports, ballet, art or anything they're involved in, will work.

4. **Let them plan meals.** Give them a couple of options for the entree and for the sides, and let them choose. As they get older and more involved with the cooking tasks, explain to them what goes into good menu choices—balancing colors, nutrient components, textures and so forth.

5. **Have Fun!** Don't be afraid to get messy or silly. Enjoy your time with the kids, whether they're yours or they're little relatives or friends. Make it memorable.

MENU

Tomato Basil Soup

Pepper Crusted Beef Tenderloin Salad
with Red and Yellow Teardrop Tomatoes,
topped with Fresh Mozzarella and Mom's Vinaigrette

Tarragon and Onion Marinated Shrimp

Garlic Accented Tuscan Toast

Crudités
with Summer Lemon Dill Crème Fraîche

Dijon New Potato and Haricots Verts Salad
with Chili Walnuts

Lime Zest Sand Tarts

Blonde Brownies

Strawberry Lemonade

Summer PICNIC

The summers in Houston are long and hot, hot, hot! Many people schedule long vacations during July, August or September to escape the heat. But some of us have to stay here and melt, so I try to create fun entertaining ideas to keep things lively. If you live in gentler climates, or if you're here and you can schedule it before the unbearable heat and humidity set in, a late afternoon picnic in your back yard is a refreshing way to entertain.

One hot summer, I decided to go with a "cool" concept for our client. We used brightly colored tablecloths, foods and décor that created a cool image for the guests,

even though the mercury was high. I found an antique milk bottle holder for one of the centerpieces, and used wine carafes as vases. Although this event was in the hostess' backyard, it would be very easy to recreate at a park or the beach.

For successful picnic and outdoor entertaining:

- Select items for your menu that enable you to do all the preparation and assembly in advance.
- Menus should not have anything that needs to be heated or contains mayonnaise.
- Keep it simple. The best picnics consist of good weather, good wine, good cheese and good company.
- Use creative serving pieces, such as sand pails, mason jars and baskets.
- Although disposable plates and flatware are easy and convenient, using bright colored ceramic plates and coordinating flatware makes the event more interesting and festive.
- Keep pesky insects and the relentless sun in mind. Have insect repellant and sunscreen in a cute basket or bucket so guests can grab it as needed.
- To keep your food at the highest quality, packaging is very important. If you are taking your picnic outside of your home, pack everything in small containers that can go into a cooler on ice or ice packs.
- Add color to your table by creating an edible centerpiece using vegetables and fruits.

DOES IT HAVE TO BE FANCY?

My tomato basil soup has very humble beginnings. About ten years ago, I was asked to cater a luncheon for 400 ladies. They wanted Tomato Basil Soup as the first course. My chef had worked tirelessly for about eight hours making the soup from scratch. She finished it about 7:00 in the evening and was comfortable that it would be chilled by morning. She insisted that I taste her wonderful creation.

Unfortunately, it didn't meet my expectations. One of our staff accidentally turned the heat on high when the soup was supposed to be simmering. The entire—enormous—pot of soup had burned and scorched. It was terrible, and very much beyond repair. We realized that we had time to make new soup before the next morning, but we didn't have another twelve hours to make it from scratch. A clever employee suggested that we buy marinara sauce—like Ragu or Prego and—put heavy cream in it. I had no choice but to try it. I kept my fingers crossed that the guests would think this new soup was acceptable. Not only did they think it was ok, at least twenty people called the office to say it was the best soup they had ever had. From that day on, we've created our tomato basil soup this same way. My mama used to say, "if it ain't broke, don't fix it." Hope you enjoy it!

ASPARAGUS

First cultivated in Greece over 2500 years ago, asparagus is the most elegant of vegetables. With three varieties, green, white and purple, asparagus can be served many ways. Green and white asparagus are the same variety grown by different methods, and purple asparagus is a different variety all together.

High in vitamin A, vitamin C, foliate and potassium, green and white asparagus have an interesting growth pattern. During the spring and summer months, each crown grows spears that appear every three to five days. During the height of the growing season, new spears appear every 24 hours.

When new stalks emerge from the ground they are light pink and quickly turn green in the sunlight, due to photosynthesis. White asparagus are grown in darkness. They're harvested before any daylight ever reaches them. Green and white taste similar, but the white are often more tender and are considered a delicacy in many countries.

Purple asparagus has a high level of anthocyanins, an antioxidant that gives them their purple color. They tend to be sweeter and fruitier, and they are more unexpected than their green and white cousins.

Prime season is April through June, but thanks to a global economy, you can find asparagus year round. When selecting asparagus, make sure that the spears are straight and without blemish. The tip of the asparagus should be firm and tightly held together.

PERFECT MICROWAVED ASPARAGUS

Take 1 pound of fresh asparagus and remove an inch or an inch-and-a-half from the bottom of the spears. Place the asparagus on a microwavable platter and leave uncovered. Microwave on high in 2 minute increments until the asparagus is just crisp/tender. Thinner asparagus take 2–4 minutes and larger, heartier asparagus take 4–6 minutes. When microwaving asparagus, and any other vegetables, be sure to heat in only 2 minute increments! Otherwise the vegetables will loose all of their water content and be dried out.

PICKING PEPPER AND PEPPERCORNS

Black: *Black peppercorns are picked before they're ripe and then dried. They have a strong flavor.*

White: *White peppercorns come from the same plant as the black, but they are ripe when they are picked and the husk is removed. They have a milder flavor.*

Green: *Green peppercorns are soft, unripe berries. Their flavor is mild and slightly sour.*

Pink: *Pink peppercorns are dried berries from the Baies rose plant. They are pungent, and slightly sweet. Some people are allergic to pink peppercorns.*

Casual Southern
Hospitality

I love the phrase, "Southern Hospitality." It brings to mind the warm, welcoming feeling I've experienced so often when I have visited friends in the South. Their graciousness, kindness and warmth are expressed not only in the way they treat me, but in the delicious, traditional—and sometimes not-so-traditional—food they lavish upon guests. I've discovered that Southern Hospitality is not limited by geography. It comes from the heart of the host or hostess, wherever they live.

Here's an example of true Southern Hospitality. Recently, The Stone Kitchen catered a wedding reception in a barn deep in the heart of Texas. The event was filled with love and all the charm of a true Southern wedding. Guests were invited to wear Suits and Boots. Even the bride donned handmade white cowboy boots with her gorgeous long dress. The ceremony took place at the family's farm, about ten miles down the road. We set up refreshments for the guests prior to the ceremony. Although we meticulously planned every part of the event, somehow we neglected to remember that we needed ice at the farm. All of the ice was at the barn for the reception. As soon as we realized our mistake, one of our staff headed back for the ice. On the way back, he made a wrong turn on the country roads and got lost. He managed to get back on track and was relieved to arrive back at the farm. But there was one small problem: in his flustered state, he forgot he was driving our box truck. He barreled through the front gate and it went right on through with him.

Oh dear, this was a big problem. The bride was scheduled to arrive in less than five minutes via horse drawn carriage. Staff and guests flurried together to whisk away the damaged gate. The wedding went on without a hitch. In the style of true Southern hospitality, the father of the bride was most gracious about his gate. Waiting for the wedding party to arrive at the reception, I was frantic. I immediately approached him to apologize for the incident. He could not have been nicer. He said, "Elizabeth, we need to focus on our guests right now. We'll worry about that gate later. Do what you do best, and let's make this a joyous occasion." His even-tempered and reassuring reaction allowed us to stay focused on our job and—as he said—do what we do best. It was a memorable reception, even without the gate.

After this experience, I began adding to my description of Southern hospitality. In addition to the sense of welcome and generosity, it's a gracious calmness that puts guests and their needs before all else. What a great lesson I learned from this father of the bride. I continue to use this attitude in my business, daily. No matter what happens, no matter how great the mistake or problem, I try to quickly and graciously resolve it and then move on to my primary focus. Getting angry won't solve any problems. It merely takes our energy away from what we do best. If something goes wrong at one of your parties, remember the father of the bride. Take a deep breath and turn your attention to making your guests feel your Southern Hospitality, wherever you live.

**M
E
N
U**

Fried Green Tomatoes
with Jumbo Lump Crab Meat Ravigote

Grilled Baby Back Ribs
Spicy Bourbon Barbecue Sauce

Whole Chicken Fried Quail

Roasted New Potato Salad with Bacon, Bleu Cheese and Lemon Zest

Orange Cilantro Slaw

White Cheddar and Chive Biscuits

Stone Fresh Fruit Salad
Peaches, red and yellow Cherries, Nectarine and Apricot
garnished with fresh Mint and Basil

Multi-Berry Shortcake
Strawberries, Blackberries,
Blueberries and Raspberries

Ice Cold Watermelon Slices

Watermelon Lemonade

Southern LUNCH BUFFET

We love our watermelon in the South. For this Southern luncheon, we decided to use a watermelon for the floral arrangements on the table. It looks fairly complicated, but it's rather simple. Select a tall cylindrical vase and then find a watermelon that is larger than the vase. Cut off both ends of the watermelon. You'll need to make your cuts far enough in so that the opening is a little wider than your vase. Take a large, long-handled spoon and scoop out all of the pulp from the melon, just like you clean out a jack-o-lantern. Reserve the pulp for the watermelon lemonade. Stand the watermelon on its end in the sink and allow it to drain for about an hour. Double-check to make sure your vase fits into the watermelon sleeve. Assemble your arrangement, then slip it inside the watermelon.

HEIGHTENED INTEREST

Using risers for your buffet not only creates depth, but also lets you display things in a variety of ways. It creates visual stimulation that keeps your guests' interest. There are many things around your house that you can use to create dimension on your table. Look around and see if you have any of the following: glass bricks, crushed granite slabs, square vases (to fill with fruits or colored rocks or place a tray upon), hat boxes, cake stands, or baskets, turned upside down.

TOMATOES AND HEIRLOOM TOMATOES

Most people think tomatoes are a vegetable, but technically a tomato is considered a fruit. The tomato can be either consumed raw or can be cooked into delicious dishes. Early in the 16th century, tomatoes were called "love apples" and were considered to be a type of berry. We now know that the pigment lycopene, the natural chemical that makes most ripe tomatoes red, may be particularly active in protecting the body against heart disease and some forms of cancer. Consider it a bonus when food is good and good for you.

The most common tomatoes these days are the traditional smooth red tomatoes and Roma tomatoes. As with apples and potatoes, many new varieties have come into the marketplace: Red, yellow, orange, green, cherry, teardrop, grape, cherub and on and on. Each variety has its own unique flavor and use.

Heirloom tomatoes, varieties that have been passed down through generations because of their dependability and outstanding flavor, have been brought back into commercial cultivation and come in all colors, shapes, and sizes. These old-fashioned tomatoes are rarely symmetrical, because they have not been agriculturally engineered to be uniform in size or shape. Heirloom tomatoes may not look pretty on the outside, but they can taste divine.

Whatever variety you need, look for firm and unblemished fruit. The height of tomato season is during the summer months, but good ones are available year round if you pick carefully. Tomatoes have the best flavor when they are allowed to ripen on the vine, but with the high demand they are usually picked very early. After you buy them, keep them outside of the refrigerator to allow the ripening process to continue, and the natural flavors will shine through.

Proscutto Wrapped Peaches with Basil, Asparagus and Figs

Individual Caesar Salads

Perfect Pizza Dough

Pizza Bianca
Mozzarella, Manchego and White Cheddar

Brie, Pear and Arugula Pizza
with Olive Oil with Black Truffle Salt

Spinach Alfredo Pizza

Mediterranean Pizza
Sundried Tomatoes, Artichoke Hearts, Kalamata Olives and Pulled Chicken,
Goat Cheese and Aged Balsamic

Classic Pizza
Hamburger, Sausage, Purple Onions, Red Bell Peppers,
Green Bell Peppers, and Yellow Bell Pepper

Frozen Tiramisu
Kahlúa® soaked Lady Fingers layered
with Chocolate Gelato, Coffee Ice Cream,
sweetened Whipped Cream and Mascarpone
topped with shaved Chocolate and diced Maraschino Cherries

Grown-Up
PIZZA PARTY

Entertaining with pizza is a great idea for people who love to cook or for a group that does not know each other well. Making pizza gives the guests an easy topic of conversation and helps break the ice. Before the guests arrive, I make the crusts in individual sizes so everyone gets to be creative in the kitchen. If time or motivation don't allow you to make your own dough, it's easy to buy frozen, thin-crust cheese pizzas and cut them into individual sizes for your guests to embellish. In the gourmet/foodie world in which we live, we've moved far beyond cheese and pepperoni. You can add whatever you can imagine to pizza. Offer your guests a generous selection of toppings: a couple of sauces, two cheeses, two to three proteins and about five or six vegetables will let everyone feel like a top chef.

Here's a list of some of my favorite pizza toppings to get you thinking:

Sauces: tomato, alfredo, pesto, olive oil, balsamic vinegar, truffle oil

Cheese: mozzarella, Parmesan, feta, goat cheese, brie

Meats: ground beef, ground sausage, grilled chicken, roasted chicken, pepperoni, Canadian bacon

Toppings: tomatoes, onions, bell peppers, mushrooms, olives, artichoke hearts, roasted peppers, sun-dried tomatoes, spinach, roasted garlic, fresh herbs, red pepper flakes, truffle salt

When one of my clients called me and asked for ideas to entertain her husband's out of town clients, I suggested this idea as a casual, interactive way to bring everyone together. We set up the kitchen island as an assembly line. Once the pizzas were cooked, we displayed them on the stovetop as a buffet that included Caesar salad and a frozen dessert. I added simple flowers and used the antique scales in her kitchen to hold a selection of vegetables that enhanced the "made fresh" look. *Buon appetito!*

Hallowed
HARVEST SUPPER

Anyone who knew my mother knew how much she loved All Hallows' Eve—otherwise known as Halloween. To her it was the celebration of the Saints that have gone before us and a day to celebrate ridding all of the evil spirits from ourselves. It was a time to be silly, to laugh and to express love for people of all ages. In my early years, she would invite everyone she knew to come by the house and enjoy a little frivolity. What started as a simple celebration developed into a wonderful annual affair that is continued in her honor to this day. If there was ever anyone who could spread happiness to all those around, it was my mother.

The meal took many forms over the years. My mother preferred to offer only black and orange foods. Later, my sister and I convinced her to add a green salad. It was always simple but yummy food. I designed this event to have simple elegance both in the design and in the menu, and a harvest feel rather than classic Halloween. Mom's cheese toast is a legend and the other items I've included were all part of her annual repertoire.

The salad and salad dressing have become a mainstay of my business. The dressing itself has had many names over the years. It was originally known as Green Bean Salad Dressing, then Funeral Salad Dressing, then Mom's Vinaigrette, Red Wine Vinaigrette and now it's officially The Stone Kitchen Vinaigrette.

The recipe came from my Great Aunt May, my Grandmother's sister on my mother's side. She developed a fabulous green bean salad, that Mom and I later renamed funeral salad. Mom always kept all the ingredients for the salad on hand in case someone died and she needed to take a condolence gift to a friend. The best part was that all of the ingredients were canned, except the salad dressing, and that was always made and kept in the refrigerator. I fell in love with the salad dressing and ate it with almost all salads or vegetables.

When I started The Stone Kitchen, Funeral Salad Vinaigrette just didn't seem appropriate, so we tried all the other names until it finally became the company's official salad dressing. I wonder if Aunt May knew her dressing and her salad would be famous one day? In honor of my mother, I've gone back to calling it Mom's vinaigrette throughout these pages.

WHY MAKE YOUR OWN SALAD DRESSING

As a culture, we've gotten used to buying everything already prepared and ready to eat. Whenever I give a talk and suggest that people make their own salad dressings, they look at me like I'm asking them to prepare to climb Mount Everest. But making salad dressings is one of the easiest and inexpensive ways to vastly improve the quality of your salads. I've provided instructions for many types in the Recipe section, and they're all super simple. Just try one, and you'll see what you've been missing. Dressings will keep in the refrigerator for two to three months, so it's effort that will provide lasting rewards.

GOURMAND SALAD

My good friend and work associate, Cynthia Lane, created this salad with all her favorite ingredients. During the early 2000's, The Stone Kitchen signed up as a team to walk in the AIDS walk, and we had to name our team. Thus, the Gourmand Gang emerged. After the walk, we met at Cynthia's house to celebrate our accomplishments. She served us this delicious salad and it's kept the name ever since. This is now my favorite salad to serve with our black bean soup and cheese toast. It is hearty and makes a nice accompaniment to these lighter items.

Family Dinners

Family meals are a very important part of my life. With the fast pace of our world, we all have great excuses to not dine together at the table. But, when I think back on my childhood, I realize that eating dinner with my family was what taught me my family's values and social skills. The time spent at the dinner table may be the only time you get to give undivided attention to your family and learn about their day. I believe that gathering the family around a table with a home cooked meal is an expression of love that creates memories for everyone involved. Education experts say that the family dinner increases academic performance, but the time spent getting nourishment and connecting with your family has a value that goes far beyond the school years. Treat yourself and your family to a heart-warming meal of comfort food. Slow down and enjoy the moment.

Nostalgic foods that bring back the comfort of childhood are different for everyone. My favorites are fried chicken and meatloaf. To me, comfort foods are those familiar foods that provide me with the warm fuzzies and sense of security from years past. These foods seem to promise that they'll right all wrongs. The warmth they create moves from your stomach to your heart and feeds your soul.

As a little girl, I was blessed to have a wonderful lady in my life named Ela. She worked for my mother's family when she was a little girl and continued to work for my family when I was young. My grandparents had all died by the time I was five, and Ela became my surrogate grandmother and my best friend. One of her favorite sayings was "All that won't kill will fatten." I've used that wisdom all of my life.

In addition to having inordinate wisdom, Ela was a gifted cook. She generously shared her love of cooking with me. I couldn't wait to get home from school and see what she had prepared for dinner. Ela had learned to cook without recipes, so when she measured something, she just poured it in her hand until "it looked right."

Because my daddy loved fried chicken, Ela would make it almost every week. And lucky for me, she taught me her secrets. I would get home from school and start begging her for a piece. She always said, "You can have one piece, a leg, so you won't spoil your dinner." There was nothing like that freshly cooked fried chicken leg straight from the cast iron skillet. Whenever I make chicken today, I remember the glorious smell in our house when Ela made her delicious chicken. Our afternoons together in the kitchen taught me more than cooking, they taught me what was important in life. The memory of Ela and the gifts she shared with me is always present, and it's made stronger when I cook certain foods for my family and friends.

MENU

Harvest Salad
Granny Smith Apples, Cranberries, Goat Cheese medallions,
and Pomegranate Seeds with Sweet Vinaigrette

Ela's Southern Style Fried Chicken

Mom's Meatloaf

Creamy Mashed Red Potatoes

Buttered Petit Pois

Okra and Tomatoes

Black Pepper Cheddar Biscuits

Ela's Gingerbread with Brown Sugar Crème Fraîche

Cinnamon Maple Pecan Baked Apples

Peach Tarte Tatin

Crumb Crust Apple Pie

Farm

For this event, the family wanted to have a casual family meal at the farm. We decided to serve in the kitchen from the stove and counter then bring everyone together at the dining table. Once dinner was over, we set up dessert both in the den in front of the fireplace and outside on the porch where the sun was setting. However you choose to bring your family together, create a pleasant and comfortable environment so they can relax and enjoy their time with each other and with you. The beauty of this meal is you can make everything ahead of time and spend more time with your family.

APPLES

When I was growing up, there were maybe two or three varieties of apples in the grocery store. And I'm not that old. Today, when you go to the grocery store there are anywhere from eight to fifteen varieties depending on the time of the year. How's anybody supposed figure out which one to eat? Here's a little cheat sheet for some of the more common varieties. If you live in apple country, please forgive me—of course you know way more than I. I'm just a girl from Texas who loves to eat and loves apples!

Apples are grown throughout the world. There are over a thousand varieties. Their colors range from yellow to bright green to crimson red. Some are tender; others, crisp. The best apples for eating and baking are Braeburn, Fuji, Gala, Golden Delicious, Granny Smith, Jonagold, McIntosh and Pink Lady. Rome Beauty is the premiere baking apple. Red Delicious is great for eating, but doesn't do as well for baking because it lacks the tartness of the other apples.

If you want to cut apples early and are concerned about them turning brown, put them in a container and cover them with orange juice. They won't turn brown, and orange juice is much less tart then lemon juice. Apple slices will hold in orange juice for up to 12 hours.

POMEGRANATES

About the size of a baseball, pomegranates have dark crimson to dark pink skins. Each fruit is packed with hundreds of seeds surrounded by a dark red pulp. The pulp is wonderfully full of flavor and the seeds are edible. Primarily grown in the Mediterranean countries and Asia, pomegranates have begun being produced in California. Pomegranates prefer areas with cool winters and hot summers. They're full of potassium, Vitamin C and antioxidants, and they add brightness and color in salads, as garnishes and as a beautiful, healthy drink.

CRÈME FRAICHE

Take a ½ cup of sour cream and ½ cup whipped heavy cream. Fold together the sour cream and whipped cream. Refrigerate until used. You can also purchase crème fraiche at specialty grocery stores.

MENU

Spinach and Artichoke Gratin

Crab and Shrimp Gumbo

Homemade Beef Vegetable Soup

White Rice

Cornbread Muffins, Griddled

Heart Salad
Hearts of Romaine, Artichoke Hearts,
Hearts of Palm, Roma Tomatoes
and Bleu Cheese with Mom's Vinaigrette

Bittersweet Chocolate and Dried Cherry Bread Pudding
with Amaretto Crème Anglaise

Fireside

SUNDAY SUPPER

Sunday afternoons are one of my very favorite times. Sunday is my day to relax, be lazy and cook at my leisure. Foods that cook all day and take little effort to manage are my idea of a great Sunday. As we come to the table, the house has filled with enticing aromas. It's a time to enjoy the pleasures and gifts of life. I always laugh that we have to stop and smell the roses even if they smell like chicken soup!

In wintertime, I like to curl up on the sofa with a good book in front of a blazing fire. I often nap with the excuse that I am watching football. On these days, dinner needs to be simple but yet very fulfilling and

heart-warming. Soups, stews and gumbos are my favorite homestyle winter meals and are best if left to simmer all afternoon. That means that I can get back to my sofa, and snoozing. The time allows the true flavors of the meats and vegetables to be released into the stock or sauce and create amazing flavors. This is a relaxing, inexpensive way to provide a hearty and nutritious meal for your family or dear friends.

Other than a little light cooking, all you'll need to do is add a salad and a little décor to your table. In this case, I used a collection of Chinese boxes to create a little interest for a very simple meal. That extra touch made my family feel how special they are to me, and I did very little work.

I highly recommend making gumbo for small groups of people. Making the roux is very simple if you are making it for eight to ten people, but it always reminds me of the time I had the (not so) brilliant idea to offer gumbo to a group of 200. Trust me, it only happened once, back when I was still cooking at my mother's house.

A roux is a mixture of flour and butter or oil cooked to a rich consistency. It's the base of many classic French sauces and is used in a great many cuisines. When beginning a roux, you heat the butter or fat and add the flour. Then you stir and stir over low heat while the mixture cooks and turns several colors. It didn't occur to me that making a roux for ten people takes about fifteen minutes, but making one for 200 in a large pot took about two hours. In addition to my arms aching so badly I wanted them to fall off, I managed to burn myself at least ten times with the hot mixture. Limit this treat to small groups, and no matter how hot the weather is, do yourself—and your arms—a favor and wear long sleeves!

HOW TO MAKE A PROPER ROUX

Follow these five easy steps to create the perfect roux.

1. *Melt ½ cup (unless a specific amount is called for) of butter or oil, I prefer butter, in a heavy skillet over very low heat.*

2. *Gradually sprinkle an equal amount of flour into the hot melted fat and immediately begin stirring.*

3. *Stir the mixture constantly until it reaches the desired color. A roux will go through several color changes as it cooks. The first color is a light brown, then a medium brown, followed by a reddish brown and then dark brown and then black if you can get it to that point without burning it. Each change of color takes about 5–7 minutes. I usually get to a reddish brown roux and then stop. Even with as many rouxs that I have made, I still cannot manage to get to a dark brown or black roux without burning it. Maybe I am a little impatient.*

4. *Once the roux reaches the desired color, remove from the heat. Continue stirring until it has cooled down a bit and there's no risk of burning.*

5. *Add herbs, vegetables, or whatever your recipe calls for, or store the roux—tightly covered—in the refrigerator for later use.*

Remember a dark roux will thicken less than light roux. If black specks appear in the roux, it has burned, and you'll have to start over. If you've made your roux ahead and refrigerated it, pour excess oil from the surface before reheating, or let it return to room temperature.

BUILDING A GREAT FIRE

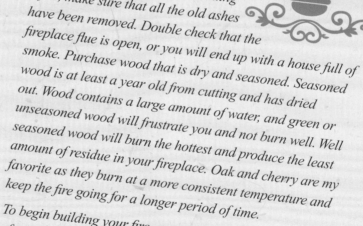

There's nothing better than a roaring fire in your fireplace. Before building a fire, make sure that all the old ashes have been removed. Double check that the fireplace flue is open, or you will end up with a house full of smoke. Purchase wood that is dry and seasoned. Seasoned wood is at least a year old from cutting and has dried out. Wood contains a large amount of water, and green or unseasoned wood will frustrate you and not burn well. Well seasoned wood will burn the hottest and produce the least amount of residue in your fireplace. Oak and cherry are my favorite as they burn at a more consistent temperature and keep the fire going for a longer period of time.

To begin building your fire, crumple up five to six sheets of newspaper and place them in the bottom center of the fireplace. Put several pieces of kindling directly on top of the paper in an overlapping criss-cross pattern. Then, place the larger pieces of wood on top of the kindling using the andirons in your fireplace to stabilize the logs. I usually start with three to four logs. Using a long match or fire starter, light the newspaper. The fire will take about five to ten minutes to get going well. Keep adding logs to the fire as the other logs burn down.

Greater Gatherings

When do you have a dinner buffet instead

of a cocktail buffet or a seated dinner? Dinner buffets are a great way to entertain when you want to offer your guests a full meal, but you don't have the room to seat everyone at a table. The best dinner buffet foods are what I call "lap friendly," meaning they are easily consumed from a plate sitting on your guest's lap. No one needs a knife. From my many years of experience, I've seen that ethnic foods work wonderfully for dinner buffets. For the foodies out there, like me, who can't decide what entrée to provide, the dinner buffet also allows you the opportunity to offer as many entrées as you like. Guests can choose what they want, and you have the fun of providing an abundance of delicious food. The following menus, Mexican and Caribbean, are good examples of the types of foods I've found work really well as festive lap foods.

MENU

Mango Margaritas
Pico de Gallo, Chili con Queso, Guacamole and Pineapple Salsa
Tortilla Chips

Texas Style Crab Quesadillas

Jose's Homemade Tomato Salsa

Mexican Mango Salad

Grilled Chicken Enchiladas
with Tomatillo Sauce

Secret Beef and Cheese Enchiladas

Mexican Rice

Charred Beans

Creamy Pralines

Fresh Fruit Sorbets
served in hollowed out fruits

Tex-Mexican

BUFFET

In Texas, we refer to our Mexican food as Tex-Mex, and of course we believe that it's the best Mexican food. Tex-Mex is just what it sounds like: Texas-style foods with Mexican flavors. Tex-Mex is a real comfort food for me. I love the unexpected explosion of flavors that come from very simple ingredients.

To me, creating a Mexican style buffet means using lots of color and texture, and having fun with it. Traditional Mexican tables are set with large wooden, ceramic and copper bowls of fruits and vegetables, such as colored peppers—fresh and dried—ears of corn, papayas, mangoes and oranges. The combination makes a gorgeous and inexpensive centerpiece. If you don't have a wooden bowl, lay a serape or other Mexican cloth on your table and arrange the fruits on it. To add depth to your centerpiece, cut some of the fruits in half and display them open. Papayas are particularly beautiful opened up, as are pomegranates, kiwi and star fruit. Oranges also work well when cut open. Using a mixture of serving trays and bowls on your buffet creates a feeling of warmth and pleases the eye.

For this event, we used the hostess' collection of Day of the Dead figurines to decorate the buffets. The Day of the Dead, *Dia de los Muertos,* is celebrated between October 31st and November 2nd, the same days as All Saints Day and All Souls Day in the United States. The Day of the Dead honors the lives of those loved ones who have gone before us.

My brother had a good friend who is a famous musician from Houston and has been producing top hits and albums since the mid 1960's. The two of them loved Mexican food, and together they developed an enchilada recipe that they were going to market to grocery stores. Unfortunately, the singer's record label would not allow them to release the product with the singer's name on it. Fortunately for me, the enchiladas were tested and tested again in my mother's kitchen. Guess who helped roll hundreds of enchiladas and was the primary taster? That's how the secret enchiladas were born, and I have the real recipe. Without question, they're the best cheese, chicken and cheese or beef and cheese enchiladas that I've ever eaten. The secret's in the sauce.

Enjoy!

CHILE PEPPERS

Chiles, or chilis, are the pungent fruit of the capsicum, also called chili peppers. The heat from a chili pepper is concentrated in the interior veins or ribs near the seed heart, not in the seeds as is commonly believed. The burning sensation that chili peppers give off comes from capsaicin—or more accurately, a collection of compounds called capsaicinoids. For hotness, size matters. In general, the smaller the pepper, the hotter it will be. All the world's most potent peppers are less than three inches long. Chilies increase your metabolism, so eat up!

__Anaheim:__ These California green chilies range from mild sweet to moderately hot.

__Chile de Arbol:__ This chile—also known as "Cola de Rata"—is often dried and toasted.

__Guajillo Chiles:__ This smooth skinned red chile is spicy. Because they're tangy and bright, they are often added to stews and soups.

__Pequin Chiles:__ These tiny dried red chiles are full of heat and have a unique flavor. Typically, the pod is dried and crumbled.

__Yellow Chile Peppers:__ There are many kinds of yellow chile peppers. The flavors range from medium-hot to hot. Some of the most well known include: Santa Fe Grande, Caribe, Banana Pepper, Floral Gem, and Gold Spike.

ROASTING PEPPERS

When you roast peppers over high heat, their skins blacken and blister. Peel it off and you'll find a sweet, tender treasure below. Any fresh pepper can be roasted, but those with thick flesh, such as bell peppers and jalapenos, work best. Using a gas stove top, turn the flame on high, and place pepper directly on the burner in the middle of the flame. Use tongs to turn the pepper every few minutes until the entire pepper is black. Remove from the heat and cool for 5-10 minutes. Place the pepper under cold running water and use your fingers to remove the black skin. An alternate method is to place the pepper under a broiler using the same procedure to achieve the crispy black skin.

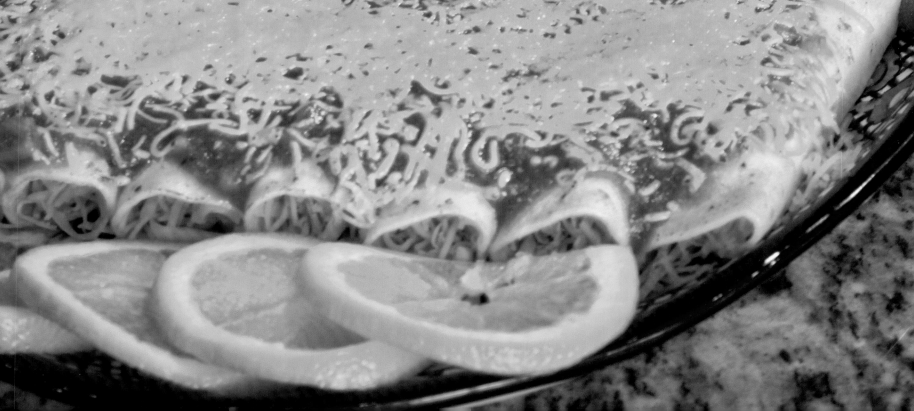

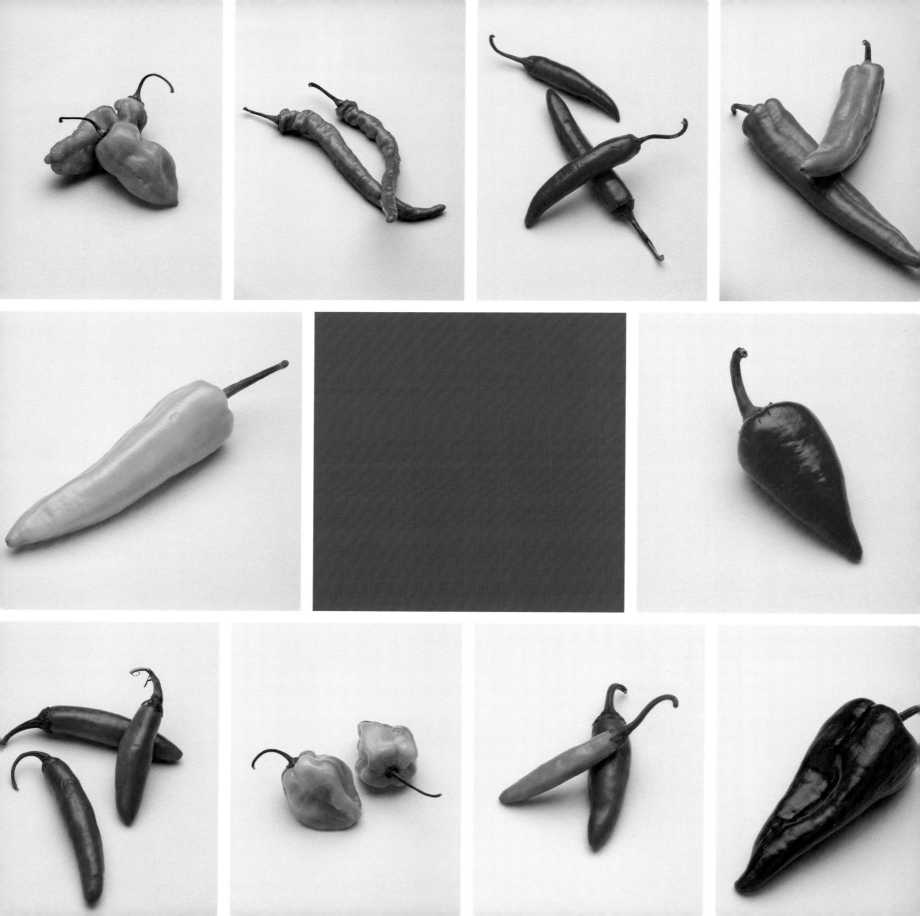

FRESH PEPPERS

All of the peppers that are red in color have high levels of vitamin C. Most peppers are also a good source of B vitamins and B6. They're high in potassium, magnesium and iron.

Bell: *These peppers are mild and sweet, great for salads and roasting.*

Poblano: *These sweet and spicy peppers are mild to medium hot. They're great for soups and for stuffing. Dried Poblanos are called Ancho or Mulato.*

Jalapeno: *These peppers are medium hot. When they are smoked and dried they are called Chipotles.*

Serrano: *These peppers are very hot and tangy. They're used in hot salsas and soups. Dried, they're called Chile Seco.*

Habanero: *Habaneros are extremely hot. They're typically used for salsas and rubs.*

M E N U

Plantain Chips with Chimichurri Sauce and Peach Salsa

Zesty Caribbean Salad
Mixed Lettuces, sliced Orange segments, Kiwi, Star fruit, Avocado,
Jerk Spice Cashews, and crumbled Bacon with Coriander Lime Vinaigrette

Plantain Crusted Shrimp
Papaya Chile Remoulade Sauce

Chili Lime Marinated Flank Steak
with Tropical Fruit Salsa

Chimichurri Grilled Grouper wrapped in a Banana Leaf

Caribbean Chicken with Lime Coconut Butter
with Hearts of Palm and Tomatoes

Grilled Sweet Potatoes, Yellow Peppers, Zucchini and Green Onions

Sweet Fried Plantains

Miss Judy's Banana Puddin' Shots

Key Lime Tartlet

Chocolate and Macadamia Nut Tartlet

Rum Cake

Specialty Beverage
Dark Rum and Tonic with Lime

Island
CRUISE

The Caribbean Islands were settled by multiple cultures over the years, and their foods reflect that diversity. The predominant spices used in Caribbean foods are jerk spice, allspice, coriander, cinnamon, nutmeg, mace, turmeric, clove and curry. Fresh ginger can be added to almost any dish from the Islands. To finish the flavor complexity, rum is added to many dishes, and is then used to make wonderfully refreshing, cooling beverages.

An Island Cruise is a great summer entertaining idea. Most of the foods will work beautifully outdoors and are cooling to the senses in the hot sun.

Very early in my career, when I was still working out of my mother's kitchen, I had a client who wanted to have an Island party for eighty people. Today, eighty is an easy, manageable number for me. Back then it was the largest party that I had ever catered. I worked on the event for months. We rented palm trees to put in the back yard around the pool. This was way before I knew how to manage the number of items that I offered, and my recollection tells me that we had about twenty different items on the buffet. It took me and five of my friends three entire days to prepare the food. Try to imagine the coolers lined up in my mother's kitchen while every pot that she owned was in constant use. It

was ultimate chaos.

Finally, the day came for the party. We had checked and double checked everything. It started to rain and I was praying it was going to pass, or we'd have to move the party inside. We finished the prep and loaded the vehicles. The rain continued. I was oblivious to how much rain had fallen until my client called me. Her pool was completely overflowing, and her street was flooding with water over the curbs. Needless to say she cancelled the party. No one could get to her house. What was I to do with all this food that was completely ready to go? Most of it wouldn't last. In the words of my mother, "The party must go on!" Even though the client didn't have her party, we had quite a celebration with all that wonderful food. Floods and all! Anyone who could navigate the waters and get to the house was invited, and Mom was right in the middle of it all. Most generously, the client rescheduled the event for two weeks later and paid me for all the food that I purchased the first time!

The event pictured here was created for a client in Galveston who entertained a group of friends by the pool. To combat the extreme heat of the summer, we developed a menu with cool foods. The flowers consisted of red ginger, heliconia, pineapple protea and orchids with banana leaves and tropical fruit on the trays. Tray garnish is an important part of entertaining. I prefer to use things that are edible and work well with the theme. Tropical fruits are one of the most colorful and festive foods to use on trays. There is a great variety, and they're just beautiful when you cut them open. Citrus fruits work well, too.

Specialty drinks are a great addition to a festive event. I try to pick ones that most people will enjoy. The drink I chose for this event was one that I first had when I went to the Bahamas with friends and is now my drink of choice: Dark Rum and Tonic with Lime. Very refreshing and delicious!

PLANTAINS

The plantain is a variety of banana that is very large and firm. It's used a lot in South American countries. When picked, it has a bright green color. Then, as it ripens, it becomes yellowish to almost black. When plantains are green, they're very firm and do not have a lot of residual sugar. They're used primarily for frying and making chips. When they are allowed to ripen, they turn almost black and become very sweet. At this stage they are cut and fried to make sweet plantains or maduros.

FRESH FISH?

The fish fillet should smell fresh and almost odorless. If you notice fishy, sour or ammonia-like smells, the filet is not fresh. Be wary if the fish looks dry, has any yellow, green or brown discolorations, or if the flesh is mushy. The flesh of the fish should be firm and spring back to the touch. If you are looking at a whole fish, the eyes on the fish should be clear and plump, and the gills should be bright red.

BANANA LEAVES

Banana Leaves are the large leaves from the banana plant. They add wonderful flavor to cooking meats and fish. They can be used to wrap fish, meats or tamales before grilling, roasting or steaming. The leaves impart a slight tropical flavor and keep the meat or fish from drying out while cooking. These leaves are available at specialty Latin American grocery or specialty stores.

Getting More *Formal*

Seated dinners are a great way to entertain

a small business group or a larger group for a festive occasion. They're generally more formal than a dinner buffet or a cocktail buffet. The classic seated dinner consists of a three course meal of a salad, entrée and dessert. You can add a soup course, a fish course, and a cheese course if you desire.

If you're thinking about hosting a seated dinner at your home, a great way to add a personal touch to your table is to incorporate a collection that you have as part of the décor on the table. In three of the following four scenarios, I have used a collection to decorate the tables. It is inexpensive and it adds some color and variety.

Recently, I was asked to participate in a charity chef dinner. Each chef was asked to prepare a five course seated served meal for ten guests who had paid $1,000 per person to attend. As you've seen, I'm a little out of the box, and I definitely like a challenge. The wonderful people who work with me are not as adventuresome. I believe it is my job to push the envelope and push their buttons just a little. What's life without a little challenge every now and then?

I decided to create the five-course meal and each course had between six and ten items or components on the plate. You guessed it: no one thought it was a great idea except me. To give you an example, the third course was the palette cleanser. It consisted of an Asparagus Vichyssoise with a Mint Crema in a shot glass on a plate. We added a scoop of grapefruit sorbet and garnished it with caramelized grapefruit, a grapefruit reduction and fresh poached ginger with fresh mint. It was a *yummy* meal. But it took five staff to plate the meal for ten people. Crazy? Yes, but it was so much fun! My suggestion to you is to choose a simpler palette for your seated dinners.

M E N U

Hors d'Oeuvres
Grilled Venison Sausage with Chardonnay Mustard
Cheese Board
Buttered Toast Points

Salad Course
Baby Spinach, Baby Arugula and Radicchio, Shaved Parmesan,
Seared Duck Breast, Orange Segments with Orange Vinaigrette and
Duck Cracklings

Fish Course
Rainbow Trout en Papillote
and Julienned Vegetables

Intermezzo
Grapefruit Sorbet

Entree
Whole Semi Boneless Grilled Quail
Fig and Morel Mushroom Risotto
Sugar Snap Peas and Pearl Onions

Dessert
Chocolate Phyllo Purses

Wild Game

WINE DINNER

Wine is a matter of personal preference. Just because a wine is expensive doesn't mean it will taste good to you. Whether you're a novice wine drinker or a connoisseur, don't be afraid to try different wines at different price levels. Tasting a variety is the only way to determine what you like and enjoy. My best advice is never let a waiter admonish you for not ordering a more expensive bottle of wine. There are many reasonably priced—even inexpensive—bottles that are delicious.

When serving a multiple course dinner, intermingle lighter and heavier courses. For example, follow a

cream soup with a light salad topped with citrus vin-aigrette. This pattern helps to avoid palette fatigue, or the dulling of your palette which renders it unable to taste flavors. Often you'll hear about palette fatigue associated with tasting many wines, but it happens with food too. The consensus is that it is not your taste buds that are overwhelmed but your brain receptors. A break in the action of wine tasting or food tasting is recommended to rest your brain and your palette. Foods, such as citrus sorbets and granitas that are highly acidic and slightly sweet, work well to refresh your palette.

Texas is known for its abundance of wild game: deer, quail, dove, wild boar, turkey and duck. Whether or not you are a hunter, game meats are widely available here, both in specialty grocery store and via the Internet.

Personally, I prefer to buy the game. I have spent my life preparing wild game shot by my clients who promise me it is de-feathered and clean of all buck shot. And I never believe them anymore. I have pulled more feathers and buck shot out of birds that I did not shoot, or even think about shooting. If your husband insists on bringing home the big catch, make him promise to get it *very* clean before he puts it on your counter to prep.

This event started in the Wine Cellar of my client's home. We served wonderful cheeses and light wines to start, and then the guests moved to the table for the served meal. The table was adorned with a collection of duck decoys, and the look was complemented by the horn-handled dinner ware and the client's Spode bird plates.

WINE WISDOM

Wine Serving Temperatures

Champagne or Sparkling Wine: around 45 degrees

Light White Wines: around 50 degrees

Heavier White Wines: around 53 degrees

Light and Medium Red Wines: around 55 degrees

Heavier or Full bodied Red Wines: around 60 degrees

Pairing Wine with Food

Pairing is not an arcane science. It is simply the decision of which wine will bring out the best in a given food, and which food will bring out the best in a given wine.

Champagnes and Sparkling Wines: pair well with soft brie style cheeses, cream-based soups, caviar, and smoked salmon.

Light White Wines: pair well with shellfish, cream-based soups, fresh fruits and vegetables. Clean flavors.

Full Bodied White Wines: pair well with semi-soft cheeses, poultry, poached fish, grilled fish, grilled shrimp, and other spicy seafood flavors.

Light to Medium Bodied Red Wines: pair well with game meat, pork, and hard sharp cheeses.

Full Bodied Red Wines: pair well with grilled meats, beef, heavy game meats, chocolate, rich sauces, and rich broths.

Chill Out

If you need to quickly chill a bottle of wine, fill an ice bucket full of ice and add water ¾ of the way up. Put the bottle in and turn it for five to seven minutes. It will emerge chilled and ready to drink.

DON'T BE AFRAID TO SERVE RED WINE

Many of my clients tell me that they don't want to serve red wine because it stains if it's spilled. Here are several solutions that really work:

White wine is the best solvent for red wine. Keep a bottle of inexpensive white wine in the fridge just for these occasions. After a red wine spill on a carpet, furniture or clothing, immediately pour white wine on it. Then, blot the area (do not rub) and the red wine should come right out. If part of the stain remains, pour table salt (regular iodized table salt) on it and the rest of the stain will come out. On carpet, Oxy based stain removers and club soda also works well.

Once at a wedding, I had a guest spill an entire glass of red wine on the bride. Tears rolled down her face, as I grabbed a bottle of white wine and led her to the bathroom. She thought I was crazy, but I convinced her that nothing could make it worse. We might as well try. In ten minutes, she was back out dancing, with no red wine on her dress.

MENU

Blue Crab Dip
with Buttered Toast Points

Pear and Amaretto Brie
served warm
with Crusty French Bread

Oven Roasted Beef Tenderloin
with Dad's Secret Sauce

Consommé Rice Pilaf

Blanched Asparagus
with Béarnaise

Curry and Bacon Broiled Tomatoes
topped with crushed Saltine Crackers

Homemade Yeast Rolls

Grand Marnier Soufflé
with Grand Marnier Créme Anglaise

The Birthday Dinner:
SET IN STONE!

Birthdays are about making the honoree feel special. Coming together to celebrate some- one's life is not only meaningful for that person; it leaves everyone involved with wonderful memories of happy times.

At the Stone household "The Birthday Dinner" was "Set in Stone," and still is. In my mother's brilliance, she selected a meal that was elegant and special but more importantly for her, simple and easy to execute. The only thing that changed was dessert. The honoree always had

the pleasure of selecting a sweet of his or her choice.

This entire birthday dinner menu, with the exception of the dessert Soufflé, can be prepared one day ahead and just heated right before the meal. For this "Birthday Dinner" the center of the table is lined with blue and white Chinese vases. They were filled with blue and white hydrangea, 'Big Fun' roses, blue delphinium, seeded eucalyptus, and snap dragons accompanied by an antique Santos collection. Although it's very simple, it makes a most impactful centerpiece.

BEEF TENDERLOIN

Beef Tender is one of the most versatile cuts of beef available. Many clients and even devoted foodies will argue with me at great length about my thoughts on beef tenderloin. Everyone has their own special way to cook tenderloin. The reality is that it is really hard to truly mess up tenderloin. Even if you overcook it, it is still more tender than other cuts of meat. I know few people who have cooked as many beef tenders as I—and my wonderful catering chefs—have. Over the last twenty years my company and I have prepared over 7500 whole beef tenders, so the experience that I have under my belt gives me a little credibility when I make these statements.

Beef Tender Credo:

- *Beef tenders are very versatile and very hard to mess up*

- *There's no need to buy top grades such as Prime or Angus, lower grades are just as tender and much less expensive (up to $15.00 per pound less)*

- *Marinating it will make it mushy after it is cooked (Beef Tender is already tender—hence the name. Marinating is primarily used to tenderize meat. If you marinate beef tender—especially in something acidic— it's going to begin to break down the tissue and will render it mushy once cooked.)*

- *Cook it very quickly on very high temperatures (Slow cooking is great for less tender cuts of meat that need long times in the oven to help make the meat more tender. Long cooking times for beef tenders just dries out the meat and makes it tougher than it should be.)*

- *Add your marinade immediately after cooking while the meat is still hot and the flavors will be drawn into the meat as it cools*

SECRET SAUCE

When I was growing up, my Daddy had a small piece of property where he raised cattle. About once every six months, he would come home with half a steer—cut into steaks and roasts, thank goodness. It was great to have the meat, but Mom was always quite overwhelmed by it. He finally had to buy a chest freezer to hold it all. Due to the abundance of meat in the house, we ate meat at least three times a week. Sunday night was Dad's night to cook and steaks on the grill were his favorite. He developed a sauce made of butter and bleu cheese and a few other ingredients that we refer to today as secret sauce. The secret sauce became a very important part of The Birthday Dinner.

Dad claimed he never told anyone what was in the recipe except for my nephew, David, who claims he will only pass it on to his son, Stone. Despite all the secrecy, I believe that I have come up with a recipe that would make my Dad proud.

HOLLANDAISE RESCUE

Both Hollandaise and Béarnaise are egg and butter-based sauces developed by the French. They are culinary mainstays in that country. I love them both. As with all beloved foods, there are many recipes for both, but in general, Hollandaise is the base sauce and all other egg and butter based sauces develop from it. For instance, with Béarnaise you add a few shallots and a little tarragon, for Maltase Sauce you add the juice of Blood oranges.

Many people are afraid of these types of sauces because they tend to break very easily. A breaking sauce is one where the butter separates from the eggs. A quick way to fix this is to add cold heavy cream and stir with a whisk or fork. The sauce will come back together.

TIPS FOR MAINTAINING SILVER

Silver is easy to maintain if you follow a few simple tips. If it's not polished on a regular basis, silver will tarnish. It will eventually turn black and you may not even recognize it as silver. To clean and maintain silver, use a silver cream, such as Wright's with a soft sponge or cloth. Make sure that you wash your silver with hot water and dry it immediately, or the water will spot the silver. After cleaning, store your silver wrapped in silver cloth or wrapped tightly in a plastic bag. Avoid touching the piece with your hands, as the oil from your hands will cause the silver to tarnish quickly. Silver cloth gloves are available that you can use to lightly polish some of your pieces or wear when you are putting your silver away.

FIX DROOPING CUT HYDRANGEA STEMS

Hydrangeas are some of the most beautiful flowers in the world but they love water and will let you know if they're not happy with the amount they're getting. There are a couple of things you can do to help the hydrangea not droop. Boil some water and then put it into a coffee cup. Cut the hydrangea to the desired length and immediately put the cut stem into the hot water for about thirty seconds. This will open up the stem and keep it from getting clogged. Then put the stem into fresh water at room temperature or in the arrangement water. If your stems do droop, I suggest placing the heads of the hydrangea down into a water bucket. Yes, I do mean the flower part. Hydrangeas will drink from their blooms. Leave the blossoms submerged in the water for several hours or overnight. Then make a fresh cut and follow the hot water method again and your hydrangea should be in great shape. I have left drooping hydrangea in water overnight and they have come back nicely.

MENU

First Course
Caramelized Duck Breast Salad
poached Bing Cherries, toasted Hazelnuts,
and shaved Parmesan,
tossed in a Thyme Balsamic Vinaigrette

Second Course
Pan Seared Sea Scallops
over Saffron Risotto in Tomato Broth

Entrée Course
Dijon and Herb Crusted Double Rack Lamb Chops
with Cabernet Demi-Glaze
Braised Baby Vegetables

Dessert
Rustic Pear Gallete
with Amaretto Caramel Sauce

Elegant
CHRISTMAS DINNER

Christmas is "The" time to entertain. If you choose to entertain during the holiday season, try to consider all the other events that occur that month. Any day during the month of December is acceptable as a date for a holiday party. Of course the most desirable days are Fridays and Saturdays, but Sunday through Thursday evenings also work well.

In the catering world, December is the height of our year. On any given Saturday evening in December we might have as many as ten events, all at the same time. It is the epitome of craziness. One year, we sent a team to an event at a client's house and forgot to send them

with any table or tray decorations and we forgot all the beverages. With eight or ten events in a night, something always gets missed, but this was extreme. The captain called and just as I happened to be leaving with Cynthia, my event planner at the time, to head to several of the events. At the time, I was driving a four door sedan. We proceeded to load all of the beverages for 250 guests in the car and then realized there was just enough room for the two of us and no room for the decorations or tray garnish. With an incredible will to succeed and take care of one of our favorite clients, we began to stack and pack all the décor and produce for garnish around Cynthia in the passenger seat. I could not see her nor could anyone else. We were laughing hysterically along the way. Once we arrived and began to unload, the captain said to

me, "Where is Cynthia?" Only then did I realize that we still needed to unload all the stuff around her and let her out. Needless to say, I have given up driving a sedan and gone back to an SUV.

Some things to consider if you're planning an event in December: If you decide to have it on a Friday or Saturday evening, realize that most likely your guests will be party hopping. It's important to invite guests for Friday and Saturday evenings over a three or four hour time frame so that they have the opportunity to go to more than one gathering. There are different ways to style an invitation in order to inform your guests of the purpose of the gathering. If you state the event time is 7–10 pm, this indicates that it is more of an open house. Guests can stop by any time between the hours

of 7 and 10. If the invitation reads 7:00 pm, this would indicate that you prefer everyone to arrive between 7 and 7:30 pm, and festivities will most likely be wrapping up by 9 or 9:30 pm. Neither is right or wrong. It completely depends on the type and style of party you want to host.

This event was a very formal family Christmas dinner. The table design was created by a professional event designer and florist. The table was covered with a dark green textured cloth and topped with translucent silk. She then added a runner of red rose petals down the center of the table and finished the look with two tall arrangements. The vases were covered with green leaves interspersed with red rose petals. This is a very innovative and dramatic technique that is fairly easy to execute. Attach the leaves to the vase using a hot glue gun. The arrangements consisted of a mixture of Pyracantha berries, red roses, red spider lilies, red Hypericum berries and antique Dutch red Hydrangea. The candle holders and place card holders were my favorite. She used hollowed out artichokes for the candles and studded them with rose petals and for the place card holders, she used a mini artichoke inside of a rose.

All of these incredible ideas and arrangements for this Christmas dinner setting were created by my friend award-winning event designer and florist, Rebekah Johnson at Bergner and Johnson Design in Houston.

RISOTTO

Rice is the most popular grain in the world. Each country has its special type of rice and a particular way of cooking it. Risotto is absolutely Italian in origin and style.

Risotto is made from short grain Italian rice called Arborio or Carnaroli. It is very different from most of our American rice. The typical rice grown in America is long grain rice that does not have as much starch in it. The short fat Arborio grains release the perfect amount of starch to yield a perfect creamy culinary treat. The general rule for risotto is first to toast the rice in butter or oil over low heat and then add hot liquid a little at a time until you have a rich and delicious mixture. The short grains absorb enormous amounts of liquid and in the process release the natural starches to make the creamy mixture. It may absorb so much liquid that you may think you have done something wrong. I had an employee call me once from an event and said I have added so much liquid that I think I have ruined the risotto, and the risotto is still very tough. I told her to just keep adding until it gets soft. She actually called a second time and I assured her that she was doing it correctly. It turned out great. Because of the type of rice and the absorption of the liquids, you can add numerous flavors to risotto to add variety to your meals. In this particular meal, I selected saffron to add flavor and color, but don't be afraid to experiment with different vegetables and cheeses.

HOW TO SCORE A DUCK BREAST

When purchasing duck breast, make sure the skin is still attached. Thaw the breast completely and marinate/season. Using a sharp knife, make small cuts into the skin and almost thru the fat layer of the skin, but careful not to slice into the breast. Make the cuts all the way across the duck in ½ going both ways to create a grid. Scoring the skin of the duck breast prevents the skin from shrinking up and pulling the breast meat into a plump ball. Scoring also allows the fat to emerge from the skin and seep into the meat to give it a wonderful flavor.

SAFFRON

Saffron is the world's most expensive spice. Coming from the dried stigmas of the saffron crocus, it takes 75,000 blossoms or 225,000 hand-picked stigmas to make a single pound which explains why it is the world's most expensive spice. Most of the time people say they cannot put saffron's flavor in words. If three people tasted saffron at the same time, all three would probably give you a different answer on how it tastes. That isn't surprising when you consider the fact that there is not one single ingredient known to us which can be substituted for saffron.

Cheers

A cocktail party is probably one of the most versatile and hostess friendly events. The traditional cocktail party spans a two to three hour time frame and offers a variety of food choices. Surely, everyone will find something they like to eat. If you are looking to create a "come and go" atmosphere, or if you have a group of people who do not know each other well, the cocktail party is your answer.

Personally, the Cocktail Party is my favorite way to entertain because I truly love a good cocktail, or maybe because I find it the easiest way to entertain. Either way, there is no style of event that lends itself as well to mingling and visiting with your guests.

Cocktail parties, as the title suggests, are cocktails served with food. The bar is an important piece of your event, and there is a general understanding that you will be offering a full mixed bar. Many of my clients state that they do not want to offer alcohol because it is so much more expensive. This is not necessarily true. Wines and beers can be very pricey, and offering a selection of items is much nicer and more accommodating to your guests. Do not feel pressured to provide as many offerings as a bar, but a small variety makes for very gracious entertaining.

Many people have built in bars in their homes and some do not. Think about the number of guests you will be entertaining and if your bar is accessible to many guests. If not, I highly recommend to many clients to move their bar to the kitchen island or to a table that is accessible.

The bar is a favorite gathering place, especially for the men. If your home bar is too close to the front door, try moving it outside on the porch or on the kitchen counter. If the bar is too close to the front door, you will create a bottle neck (too many people trying to get through a narrow space) with your guests. Cheers!

PORTIONING YOUR BAR: PER 50–75 GUESTS FOR 3 HOUR EVENT

1 liter Vodka
1 liter Scotch
1 liter Bourbon
1 liter Gin
1 liter Rum
1 liter Vermouth
6 (750 ml) Bottles Red Wine
6 (750 ml) Bottles White Wine
1 Case Light Beer
1 Case of Regular or Imported Beer
4 (32 oz) Bottles Tonic
4 (32 oz) Bottles Club Soda

12 pack Coca Cola
12 pack Diet Coke
12 pack of Sprite, 7up or Ginger Ale
1 (32 oz) Bottle Orange Juice
1 (32oz) Bottle Cranberry Juice
8 Limes
4 Lemons
1 Orange
1 Bottle of Cocktail Olives
1 Bottle Cocktail Onions
1 Bottle of Maraschino Cherries

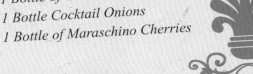

This will cover most cocktails requested in someone's home.

**M
E
N
U**

Hors d'Oeuvres

Kentucky Cheese Bisque with Candied Bacon and Citrus Crème Fraîche

Southern Chicken Tender Sliders on Buttermilk Biscuit
with Micro Greens and Peach Preserves

Blue Crab Salad with Orange Mayonnaise on Wonton Crisps

Kentucky Slow Roasted Pulled Pork with Raspberry Chipotle Sauce

Turkey Hash in Puff Pastry Cups

Cheddar Cheese Grits Soufflé

Spinach and Swiss Cheese Egg Casserole

Bacon Scones with Sweet Corn and Tomato Salad

Tomato Pie

Bread Pudding with Maker's Mark Bourbon Sauce

Pecan Tassies with Bourbon Clotted Cream

Mint Juleps

Kentucky

DERBY

Horse racing in Kentucky dates back to the late 1700s. One hundred years later, the Kentucky Derby was founded at Churchill Downs. It has served as the location for the Blue Ribbon of horse racing since 1875.

The Garland of Roses, Mint Juleps and Big Hats provide strong foundations for a great party around the Kentucky Derby. The red rose has been the official flower since 1904. The winning horse dons a garland of 554 red roses sewn into a green satin backing. Since 1938, the Mint Julep has been the official beverage of the Derby. Over 120,000 Mint Juleps are served every

year at the Derby. So, red roses and a Silver Goblet filled with a mint julep: what else do you need?

It's all about the hat. Hats are part of the spectacle, and the spectacle is a big part of the Kentucky Derby. There are no rules for Derby hats. They come in all sizes, all shapes and all colors. Whatever you do for your Kentucky Derby party, make sure that you request that your guests wear hats.

There are many foods that are synonymous with the Derby. Kentucky ham, biscuits, fresh fruit and the ubiquitous pulled pork. I've included a recipe for pulled pork that is relatively easy to prepare. But, don't get over ambitious and try to cook it for lots of people. The

first time a client asked me for pulled pork, it was for a party of 500. Being the crazy person that I am, I agreed to make it. No challenge is ever too big. But then again, I won't tell you what my staff had to say about it. I was clueless about the secrets of pulled pork. I knew slow smoking was the key—for twelve to fifteen hours. Sure, I thought, no big deal. I have a smoker at my house. Well, I had a large smoker for a home, not for 350 pounds of pulled pork.

Then, I had the bright idea of renting a four-door smoker, and a good friend volunteered to help with the project. It reminded me of the early days of my catering, but this was actually just a couple of years ago. It took us all night and most of the next day to get all that pork cooked. And after it's cooked, it has to be wrapped in foil to cool and only then pulled.

We ran out of smoking wood in the middle of the night. We had to start putting a lot of the meat into the two ovens in of my house to finish cooking. My entire life smelled like smoke. The odor lasted for two weeks.

Fortunately, I learned a great lesson. Smoked pork for twenty to fifty people, but not for 350 unless you have the proper equipment. Lucky for me, I have since met a wonderful man in Houston who makes the best pulled pork with raspberry sauce. Thanks to Al Marcus my house doesn't smell like a barbecue shack anymore.

SILVER HALLMARKS

Silver hallmarks are markings that were used by silversmiths to prove the authenticity of their creations. Hallmarks provide conclusive identification for extremely popular pieces that were easily copied. Most hallmarks are applied by the hammer and punch method. Hallmarks are small symbols that demonstrate the brand, the quality and the age of the silver.

FOODS THAT TARNISH SILVER

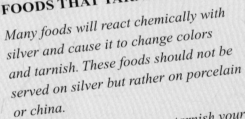
Many foods will react chemically with silver and cause it to change colors and tarnish. These foods should not be served on silver but rather on porcelain or china.

Some of the foods that can tarnish your silver include deviled eggs, asparagus, citrus fruits (such as oranges, grapefruit and lemons), mayonnaise, salad dressings and onions.

MENU

Orange and Pomegranate Granita
with candied Orange Peel
offered with choice of Vodka or Rum

Ice Watercress Vichyssoise

Chilled Seafood
Stone Crab Claws
Marinated Blue Crab Salad
Cold Boiled Shrimp

Grilled Oysters on the Half Shell
with Sautéed Grapefruit and Baby Basil

Sauce Selection
Spicy Red Sauce, Louie Sauce,
Cajun Remoulade, and Tartar Sauce

Roma Halves with Diced Heirloom Tomatoes, Avocado and Jicama Salad
drizzled with a Champagne Vinaigrette

Watermelon, Peaches and Blueberries

Crusty French Bread

Lemon Blueberry Bars
with Lemon Zest Glaze

Short
PLATES

Short plates are all the rage these days, both in restaurants and entertaining. Short plates trace their lineage back to Spain. The Spanish people have been eating small plates—called tapas—since the time of King Alfonso X, who was believed to have a disease that forced him to eat small meals and small sips of wine throughout the day. Once cured, he ordered the country to never serve wine without small amounts of food. Another legend has it that the field workers of ages past had to eat small meals throughout the day with a small amount of wine to keep up their strength. The sweetness of the wine would attract flies to their

glasses. In an effort to detract the flies they would put their plates on top of their glasses of wine. In Spanish, "tapar" meant to top. Thus, the tapa was born.

A short plate—or tapa—is simply a small portion of food that if served as a larger portion would be an entire meal. Short plate entertaining allows your guests to enjoy a variety of different foods without being too full. If you are doing a wine tasting, this is a wonderful way to serve food. You can pair wines with each course, if you like.

Here's an event we did for a group of ladies in Lexington Kentucky. The concept was to teach the ladies how to be comfortable experimenting with herbs in different formats. Now of course, with my big vision— or craziness as my staff might tell you—I selected eight different courses for a party of fifty women. Being more realistic, I might suggest you select five courses for ten to twenty guests. However grand your vision, make sure that you're excited about the food you serve your guests. I made so many new friends in Lexington, and our time together inspired me to continue to share my own love of cooking and entertaining. It was a wonderful example of the reciprocity of hospitality: when you entertain with your whole heart, you receive so much more than you have given.

FROM CRUMB-Y TO CREATIVE

As with any catering event, the best laid plans can be foiled at any given second. As I told you, I had traveled to Lexington to do this event. There was such an abundance of food that I would need to prepare upon my arrival that I tried to pre-prepare a few items and take them with me. I was confident that the biscuits would make the trip and would take one labor-intensive item off my plate. I carefully packed my equipment, my special spices and my biscuits in one bag. To my great surprise, when I finally got to the hostess's home and opened my bag, the biscuits had been jostled so much by the bumpy airplane ride, they had turned back into biscuit meal. It was not a pretty sight. Not only were they all crumbly, they had exploded from their package all over my bag.

Now what to do? There was no time or equipment to remake the biscuits. Remember what Julia says: never apologize. As I was preparing the rest of the food, I had a brainstorm: I would melt butter and pour it over the crumbles. Then, I'd toast them in the oven, and instead of serving the biscuits on the side of the soup, I'd garnish the soup with toasted buttered chive biscuit crumbs.

It was a huge hit. The toasted biscuit crumbs were so delicious, I barely had enough to serve—my helpers would not stop nibbling on the crumbs. My motto, "Butter can fix anything" proved itself once more. Perhaps actual biscuits might have been nicer, but in a pinch you have to be creative.

GROW YOUR OWN

Experiment with growing herbs in your garden. They're very easy, and most of them grow well in pots. Herbs tend to like lots of water, but they don't like their feet wet, meaning plant them in well draining pots so that the roots do not sit in water. Water them generously, but don't flood them. I find it is easier to grow herbs that have already begun to sprout rather than planting seeds. Most grocery stores today sell herbs in pots. Buy a couple and see what happens.

COOKING WITH HERBS

Even though I've been cooking for decades, I'm always looking for new information. So many more foods are available these days, and other cultures' recipes and ingredients are easily accessible. I love learning new things about food, even old favorite ingredients. Here's some information about herbs that I picked up from Mountain Valley Growers:

Chives: *Chives are best used fresh. They can be chopped fine and added to butters, soft cheeses, and salads. Bright purple chive flowers make an eye-catching and flavorful garnish sprinkled on salads, omelets, chicken and vegetable dishes.*

Oregano: *Use oregano for herbal marinades or add it (near the end of cooking) to any tomato-based sauce, sauté, stir fry, or egg dish. Fresh or dried oregano can also be combined with other herbs to make an herb crust blend for pork chops, tenderloins or chicken breasts.*

Rosemary: *As rosemary flavors our food, it also perfumes our home. Rosemary is delicious in bread or grilled with meat, and it makes a beautiful garnish.*

Sage: *Besides the traditional use in stuffing, sage is good with pork, sausage, other meats, and cheese. It is often combined with thyme and used with beans and in soups. I love to sauté fresh sage in butter. It is wonderful.*

Tarragon: *Tarragon is sumptuous with meats, and vegetables. Its slight sweetness makes it perfect for rice, pasta and dessert dishes. It can be used alone or in conjunction with other herbs, like basil, to flavor white wine vinegar.*

Thyme: *Thyme leaves may be small, but they pack a powerful punch. Thyme is one of the savory herbs, which are main course herbs used to flavor hearty meals, bone warming soups, and piquant sauces. Thyme has a warming flavor that is perfect with "winter-thyme" treats like baked butternut squash.*

HOW TO FRY VEGGIES OR HERBS

Vegetables: When breading veggies—or anything—the rule is: dry sticks to wet and wet sticks to dry. Wet and wet doesn't work; dry and dry doesn't work. In order to get your breading to stick on your veggies, first pat them as dry as possible. Then, dredge them in a bit of seasoned flour. Next, dredge the vegetables in a wet batter—either an egg wash or egg-buttermilk combination. You can also try a tempura batter consisting of 1 cup ice water, 1 egg, 1 cup flour and a splash of club soda. After the wet batter, dunk the veggie in some panko (Japanese breadcrumbs) or other fine, dried, seasoned breadcrumbs. I recommend deep frying for fried veggies, since the outer coating tends to burn if they sit in a hot pan. If you're going to pan fry, use about ½ inch oil, keep your heat moderate and be very gentle when turning them.

Herbs: To fry herbs you need ½ cup of olive oil, and ½ cup of the fresh herb you would like to fry. Make sure the herbs are clean and thoroughly dry. Place the oil into a small fry pan or pot, and heat it over medium heat. Once the oil reaches 275 to 300ºF, use a slotted spoon to lower the herbs into the oil. Be careful of any splattering oil. Fry them for about 5 to 10 seconds until they become even in color. Transfer to a plate lined with paper towels to drain.

FIGS

Figs are a tree-grown fruit with sweet flesh and tiny seeds inside. The entire fruit is edible. Fresh figs are available from mid-summer to mid-fall. Figs are best when fresh. They work well in salads or braised with meats—especially game. Their sweetness balances the "gaminess" of wild game. Kadota figs are small to medium in size and relatively sweet. They usually have green skin and a light colored flesh. The most popular figs—Black Mission—are small in size and packed full of sweetness and flavor. Brown Turkish Figs are larger than the Kadotas and have a darker more violet-colored flesh. They are equally sweet but have a spicier flavor. The green figs taste a little lighter than the darker types of figs, but you can use them interchangeably.

MARIE ANTOINETTE CHAMPAGNE GLASSES

Tall, thin Champagne flutes are well-proven to be the best serving glass for Champagne, because they preserve the bubbles and delicate aromas. So why do some people use wide-brimmed glasses?

One story—and there are several—is that back in the days of the French aristocracy, Marie Antoinette was quite in love with Champagne. Adored by her royal friends for her fine figure, she even had serving ware patterned after her anatomy. Sevres was well known for its porcelain, and she had bowls to serve food shaped from her bosom. Marie felt that her breast would make a perfect mold for drinking Champagne. While an original mold for a breast cup, is preserved in the Musée National de Céramique-Sèvres, the actual coupe Champagne glass predates the narcissistic queen of France.

Annual Celebrations

Annual Celebrations bring families to-gether. At the center of our family's holidays there is always a celebration meal. The four holidays we traditionally celebrate together are Easter, Thanksgiving, Christmas and New Years. Each family has its own holidays that are special. Whether your special holidays are listed here or you celebrate others, give your family the gift of a special meal prepared with love from your heart. Include foods that are the same every year, and introduce new surprises to keep things fresh. Pull out all the stops and create a gorgeous table. The moments we take the time to make special are the ones that we all remember most.

M E N U

Grapefruit Prosecco Sparkler

St. Andre Cheese
with Fresh Fruits, Breads and Crackers

Melon Salad
with Lavender Syrup

Cold Whole Poached Salmon
served with a Dill Crème Fraiche, Cucumber scales,
and a White Wine Dijon Mustard

Deviled Eggs with Pancetta and Crispy Onions

Leg of Lamb Boneless Herb de Provence Crusted
(served room temp)
with Mint Preserves
and sautéed Bing Cherry and Kumquat Compote

Wild Rice Salad

Goat Cheese and Tarragon Biscuits

Marinated Asparagus Tips, Snow Peas, Artichoke Hearts and Radishes
served with a Maltaise Sauce

Spring Berry Trifle

Chocolate Caramel Ganache Pops
rolled in a Cayenne Pumpkin Seed Brittle

RADISHES

Radishes are actually the root of a mustard plant: hence, their spiciness. They come in a variety of colors; red are the most common, but you can find radishes in pink, white and purple. Most radishes have a similar flavor and increase in spiciness as they age. They are usually consumed raw, but are also good roasted in the oven with salt. They will stay fresh and crispy for up to five days if you cut off the stem and any leaves and keep them in ice water.

LAVENDER

Lavender—that wonderful aromatic herb —is a cousin of mint. Its leaves are tender and long and when it blooms, it produces beautiful pale purple flowers. The flower pieces are used in Herbs de Provence, in other spice mixes and in salads. You can use the leaves to flavor a tea or delicate syrup. To make lavender syrup, make a mixture of equal parts water and white sugar. Place in a sauce pot and bring to a boil. Allow to boil for 2–3 minutes. This is simple syrup. Allow the mixture to cool slightly, and add the lavender leaves. Let them steep for 15–20 minutes. Remove the leaves and serve. Yum!

M E N U

Blonde Bloody Mary's
with Pickled Okra and Celery

Oven Roasted Turkey
stuffed with herbs, onions and oranges

Cranberry Orange Relish

Homemade Brown Gravy

Southern Cornbread Dressing

Scalloped Oysters

Harvest Squash Casserole

Whipped Sweet Potatoes
served in an Orange Cup
topped with toasted Pecans

Haricot Verts Bundles
with Chive ribbon

Homemade Yeast Rolls

Fresh Pumpkin Pie

Bourbon Pecan Pie
all served with Whipped Cream

Thanksgiving Lunch
SEATED BUFFET

I love Thanksgiving. It's such a heart-warming celebration of both the harvest provided to us by God and of family. Since the early 1600s at the Plymouth Plantation, the gathering of family and friends was the sole purpose of expressing gratitude and giving thanks to God for His harvest has occurred.

Sharing bountiful food has always been a central part of the event.

The harvest festival table would be lacking without the renowned turkey as a centerpiece. While pumpkin pie was a latter day invention, the Pilgrims and the Wampanoags did eat turkey along with other meats at their first feast, a celebration that lasted for days and included several meals. Turkey remains the mainstay of the Thanksgiving table today.

As a celebration of the harvest, there are so many wonderful things to use for a table centerpiece. The classic cornucopia is a favorite base piece. This symbol of abundance was traditionally made from a curved goat horn and now has been replaced with a similar shaped basket, or a grapevine wreath would work well also. Great elements for the centerpiece are fresh fruits such as pomegranates, crab apples, grapes, pears, apples, figs, dried corn, and colorful peppers. Hypericum berries come in a variety of colors that work well as a filler for these bountiful arrangements, along with citrus fruits and nuts.

THE RIGHT WAY TO DO THANKSGIVING

Many people have theories about "The" way to cook a turkey. Our family gave up a decade ago arguing about who makes the best turkey. Instead, everyone who wants to cook a turkey brings one. One is fried, the other baked and one roasted in a bag. Honestly, they all taste pretty much the same to me. What I live for on Thanksgiving is the left over turkey sandwich at the end of a long day. My idea of Thanksgiving heaven is sliced turkey breast with mayonnaise and a dash of Crazy Salt on toasted Pepperidge Farm thin white bread.

The other major family argument that develops each year in many houses, including ours, concerns the cranberry sauce. Really, are they all so different? My brother and nephew must have theirs out of the can, with the can ridges showing. I prefer a cranberry orange relish that my mama used to make and I have included in the Recipes. In addition to these, we have a whole berry cranberry sauce, a fresh cranberry and orange sauce and one or two others. This is a crazy amount of cranberry, but it keeps everyone happy and prevents arguments. Blending families at holiday time can be difficult—not because of the personalities but because of the different traditions. Our family has adopted peace as the theme of the day, so we just let everyone bring whatever makes them happy. Life is too short to argue about cranberry sauce.

CRANBERRIES

Cranberries are shiny dark red berries that grow on low creeping vines in wet, marshy bogs. The berries start out small and white and turn their distinctive bright red color when they ripen. To harvest the berries, the cranberry beds are flooded with about six inches of water. Ripe berries float and the flooding makes it easier to collect them. Cranberries like the cool of the Northern states and Northern Europe. Massachusetts, Wisconsin, Washington and Oregon produce the most cranberries. The harvest takes place only once per year between September 1 and November 1. Cranberries can be eaten raw, but they are so acidic that most of them are turned into juice or preserves.

GETTING PAST GRAVY ANXIETY

Lots of people I run into are afraid of gravy, or should I say afraid of making gravy. Gravy is one the simplest of sauces to make; it just requires a little patience and few easy tricks. Merriam Webster defines gravy as a sauce made from the thickened and seasoned juices of cooked meat. Food Lover's Companion says it's a sauce from meat juices, thickened with flour, cornstarch and a liquid. So how does all that translate for us as home cooks? I define gravy as a mixture of flour and butter with liquids cooked off the meat. Or, you can cheat and use canned stocks or broths. Here's what you do:

Take 2 tablespoons of butter, 2 tablespoons of flour and 3 cups of chicken stock.

I love the flavor of butter, but you can use oil if you prefer. I greatly dislike the flavor of cornstarch, so I never use it. In a heavy bottomed sauté pan, over medium heat, stir the butter and flour until the butter is melted. Continue to stir (this is the most important trick—never stop stirring) until the mixture begins to change colors. This is where the patience comes in. Sometimes it takes a few minutes. If you turn up the heat, you will burn it—so just relax and stir. Continue with this process until the sauce turns a nice golden brown. Of course, this is just a basic roux, so yes, you can continue to cook it until it becomes dark brown. Once the color is golden or medium brown, remove the pan from the heat. Add the desired liquid, very slowly. The drippings from the turkey make wonderful gravy, but so does canned chicken broth. The real trick is adding the liquid slowly, slowly, until it's all incorporated into the mixture. To finish, season the gravy with salt and pepper to taste.

SWEET POTATOES

Sweet potatoes are one of my favorite foods. They are filled with fiber, and vitamins A and C. There are many varieties of the tuber. The most common is Covington, the dark skinned one with the yellow orange flesh that is sweet and moist after cooking. Sweet potatoes can be eaten right out the oven with a little salt and butter, or they are wonderful whipped or sautéed with lots of butter, brown sugar and pecans added. I used to think of sweet potatoes only at Thanksgiving, but now I eat them year round.

AFTER THE FEAST

Part of the fun of Thanksgiving is lingering at the table, listening to stories of times past. In our family, we love to recount the story of an anonymous family member who almost burned down the house cooking the apple pie in a paper bag. The worst part was that someone used the fire extinguisher to put it out and ruined the pie. Then there was the turkey that my mother left in the oven for 12 hours. When we moved it to the platter, all the meat slid right off the bones. It was without question the ugliest turkey I have even seen, but also the best tasting. It was moist and full of flavor. What do you do when your turkey pulls an unexpected trick like that? Just smile as my mother did, and say, "Well, that's exactly what I intended!".

Baked Brie
with Port poached Figs and crisp Bacon

Red Wine Poached Cranberry Salad
with Feta Cheese and toasted Pecans,
topped with a Cranberry Vinaigrette

Hazelnut Coffee Crusted Rib-Eye Roast
with a Cabernet Black Truffle and Morel Reduction

Scalloped Potatoes with Granny Smith Apples

Sautéed Green Beans Almondine

Roasted Acorn Squash Halves
with a Maple Butter

Pomegranate and Balsamic glazed Carrots
with toasted Hazelnuts

Redwine and Cinnamon Pears with Crème Anglaise

Chocolate Pistachio Peppermint Bark

Croquembouche

Hot Wassail

Christmas Eve

DINNER BUFFET

All families have different traditions for the holidays. The family, whose gathering is pictured here, chose to celebrate at their farm by the lake. We created a rustic style event and even moved some of the furniture and big pillows outside to enhance the "comfort" theme. We wanted every aspect of the gathering to focus on allowing the family to relax and enjoy one another after the hustle and bustle of the holiday season. Although the menu is formal, I presented it in a way that the guests could eat at their leisure, exchange their gifts and take in the company and the view.

The holiday season brings a variety of natural items to use for decoration. Some great ideas are cinnamon sticks, crab apples, pomegranates and kumquats. I love to use items with rich colors, aroma and texture. We assisted the family and wrapped the packages in simple butcher block paper with raffia ribbon.

Enjoy the holiday!

SURVIVING THE MADNESS

In the catering business, the month of December is clearly utter chaos. We are running from one event to the next. It becomes so crazy during this time that truly none of us know whether we are coming or going. As I approach Christmas Eve, I am excited that the turmoil will soon come to an end, and the true reason we gather and celebrate Christmas will begin.

One year we were catering an event for long-time clients who had asked us to provide the flower arrangements for the seating tables along with everything else. About a week prior to the event, they changed their minds and said they would provide the flowers. When we arrived at the event, there had clearly been a miscommunication. There were no flower arrangements. This may seem like a small problem, but on a Saturday night in December finding someone to make four arrangements in one hour is pretty much impossible. Fortunately in Houston, most of the grocery stores sell flowers. I grabbed my clippers and ran off to the grocery store with one of my employees. She purchased the flowers and vases as I grabbed cranberries and other fruits to put in the arrangements. Then, as we headed to the event, I turned the back of the car into a florist's shop. It looked like a tornado was occurring in the car. As we stopped at lights along the way, people were gawking. The good news? The arrangements looked festive, and the client was thrilled to have them on the table. I still don't know where the confusion occurred but I can rest assured knowing that if necessary I can arrange on-the-go. As our motto says: "whatever it takes," and that we did! I can't say that those were the prettiest arrangements I ever made but, they certainly made the party look pretty. None but the catering staff and the client had any idea how they came to be.

HOW TO MAKE A CARAMEL SAUCE

Making your own caramel sauce from scratch is easier than you might think, and it takes practically no time at all. My one note of caution is to be extra careful while you are cooking the sugar, as you should with any candy making process. Once the sugar has melted it has a much higher temperature than boiling water.

All you need is one cup of sugar, six tablespoons of butter, and a half of a cup of whipping cream. Heat the sugar on moderately high heat in a heavy-bottomed 2- or 3-quart saucepan. As the sugar begins to melt, stir vigorously with a whisk or wooden spoon. When the sugar comes to a boil, stop stirring. The liquid sugar should be dark amber in color. Immediately add the butter to the pan. Whisk until the butter has melted. Once the butter has melted, take the pan off the heat. Count to three, then slowly add the cream to the pan and continue to whisk to incorporate the cream.

When you add the butter and the cream, the mixture will foam up considerably. This is why you must use a pan that is at least 2-quarts (preferably 3-quarts) big. Whisk until the caramel sauce is smooth. Let it cool in the pan for a couple of minutes, then pour it into a glass mason jar and let it cool to room temperature.

MUSHROOMS

Mushrooms are largely interchangeable in recipes, but each one has its own unique aroma and fragrance. When cooked with foods, mushrooms add an earthly element. Mushrooms are 90% water and high in phosphorous. When you're buying mushrooms, try to select ones that are firm to the touch and without bruises. White mushrooms or Agaricus mushrooms are the most common variety. Check under the cap of the mushrooms. If the skin of the underside of the cap is still attached to the stem, you know they are very fresh.

Wild mushrooms can be found in many wooded areas. Unless you are a professional mushroom harvester, leave the picking to the pros. Many mushrooms may resemble safe mushrooms, but can be poisonous.

These mushrooms are readily available in grocery stores:

White Mushroom: *This type of mushroom is also known as the button mushroom. Although called a white mushroom its color ranges from white to light brown. It comes in a variety of sizes from about 1" in diameter to almost 4" in diameter. It is widely available and its versatility makes it very easy to use when cooking or raw. The flavor will intensify while cooking. I use this mushroom in Beef Bourguignon and in my Chicken Crepes Provence.*

Shiitake: *This mushroom is also known as the Fragrant mushroom, Chinese Black mushroom, Oak Mushroom or even the Black Forest mushroom. They range in color from tan to light brown and have an umbrella type lid. They have a very rich meaty type flavor. I love to use Shiitakes in risotto or simply sautéed in butter and served on top of a steak.*

Porcini: *These mushrooms remind me of a classic toad stool and have a very distinct aroma. They are also meaty and very rich. As they are most expensive, use carefully and they also come dried. One of my favorite Porcini recipes is to make a red wine butter sauce and allow the Porcinis to infuse the sauce—fabulous over a grilled rib-eye steak.*

Morels: *Morels are prized by many cooks. They are very expensive but the good news is that a little goes a long way. Their color is dark brown and they have a dimpled top. They can be purchased fresh during the summer months and are sold dried the rest of the year. Morels are a cousin of the truffle. They have an earthy and smoky flavor profile, as well as some nuttiness. Morels add a wonderful flavor to a cream sauce over pan sautéed veal medallions. Yummy!*

TRUFFLES

This fungus is one of the most expensive and most prized ingredients in the world. Truffles grow underground near the roots of oak, chestnut and hazel trees. They are very difficult to find. Truffle farmers have pigs and dogs that do the work for them because the animals have keen sniffers and are able to locate them more easily than humans. As far back as the ancient Greek and Roman cultures, truffles were believed to have healing and aphrodisiac qualities.

There are many varieties of truffle, but the most coveted are black diamond truffles from France's Perigord region and Italy's Umbria region. White Alba truffles are from the Piedmont region of Italy. The black truffles have a pungent, earthy aroma and are usually served cooked, while the white truffles are more subtle. They have a hint of a garlic aroma and are often eaten raw. Although truffles are very expensive, it does not take many to flavor an entire dish. Black truffles are most often used to flavor sauces, risottos and egg dishes, and white truffles are grated raw over pasta dishes. Store fresh truffles wrapped in a paper towel in a plastic baggie in the refrigerator. They can also be frozen but will lose some of their flavors. To freeze, wrap in plastic, then in foil and put in a air tight baggie. To clean truffles, wipe with a damp cloth. Some people store truffles in dry white rice. This really does not help the truffle. It will draw out moisture and flavor. If you do this, cook the rice and serve with the truffles. Fresh truffles are available at specialty produce markets, or online from specialty stores such as Dean and Deluca or Sur La Table on a seasonal basis. The white truffle season lasts a couple of months usually beginning in October. The black truffle season begins in December and lasts until February. At almost $3000 per pound, think carefully how you want to use them. One ounce of truffle is a lot. A quarter or even an eighth of an ounce will allow you to add flavor to many dishes in a week's time. They are very perishable and must be kept refrigerated.

Stone Cold Caviar:
A selection of Caviars served in hand crafted Ice Blocks
Crème Fraiche, Riced Eggs, minced Onions, and Lemon wedges
Russian Buck Wheat Blini and buttered Toast Points

Variety of chilled Vodkas

Chardonnay Poached Lobster Tails, Stone Crab Claws and Shrimp
served on cocktail forks with Sage Butter

Fondue Cheese Shooters
with Cubed Bread and Granny Smith Apple Skewers

Sauvignon Blanc Wine

Beef Tenderloin Carpaccio
drizzled with Black Truffle Oil,
served with minced Red Onions and Microgreens

Toast Points

Malbec Wine

Chocolate Dipped Strawberries

Chambord Truffles

Brownie Cake Bites dipped in Chocolate

Raspberry Buttercake Squares dipped in White Chocolate

Fresh Strawberries and Raspberries with Romanoff Sauce

Rose Champagne

New Year's

EVE

How many times have you been so excited about New Year's Eve only to be oh-so-disappointed with its anticlimactic nature? After one too many of those let-downs, I decided to take matters into my own hands and do what I love to do most: celebrate with close friends and family over a wonderful meal and great wine. Regardless of the hype going on all over town about the arrival of the New Year, an exciting dinner with friends and family is always a hit.

New Year's can be fun if you decide to make it fun. For this particular party, the hostess wanted a more formal atmosphere with some over the top foods and experiences. I always remind my clients that formal does not mean stuffy. The menu I designed was intended to tantalize the guests' taste buds.

Our taste buds can distinguish five different types of flavors: sweet, salty, bitter, and sour as well as the newest discovered taste, umami—the woodsy and earthly flavor from mushrooms and truffles, or the fermentation of soy sauce and the aging of Parmesan cheese. The balance of all five of the sensors creates a harmonious explosion in your mouth. I created this menu to consist of four parts that all can be put out in the beginning of the evening. Each section is paired with a beverage to create a little fun in moving around the table.

As the old year passes away, stay home. Bring in the people you love the most and delight them with new tastes. Blow horns at midnight if you like, or go to bed early. The New Year will be enriched by the memories you create around the table.

Auld Lang Syne my friends!

CAVIAR

People have been eating caviar for at least 2000 years. Caviar comes in many varieties, shapes and sizes. Fresh caviar from the Caspian Sea sturgeon is the most prized in the world and is very costly. Fresh caviar can be held in the refrigerator for up to four weeks unopened. It should be placed in the coldest part of the refrigerator. Once it is opened, it should be consumed immediately. The eggs will break down if they are frozen and spoil at temperatures above 45 F.

Imported Caviars

Beluga: *Beluga caviar is one of the most sought after caviar because of its smooth texture and buttery taste. The egg color ranges from very black to dark grey and they are harvested from the beluga sturgeon fish. As of 2004, the US Fish and Wildlife Service declared the beluga sturgeon endangered, thus Beluga is no longer available in the United States legally.*

Ossetra: *Ossetra caviar comes from the ossetra sturgeon fish and is considered by some to be better then Beluga. The eggs range in color from light golden brown to dark brown, and tend to be large and firm in texture. The flavor of Ossetra is nutty and fruity.*

Sevruga: *Comes from the sevruga sturgeon and its eggs tend to be small and gray in color. The flavor is slightly sweet and salty at the same time.*

American Caviars

White Sturgeon: *The American white sturgeon is very similar the ossetra sturgeon. The eggs of the white sturgeon are shiny and almost black, and their flavor is nutty and buttery. The white sturgeon are grown mostly in California.*

Paddlefish: *American paddlefish come from the Mississippi and Tennessee Rivers. It is similar in taste to the sevruga sturgeon. The eggs are silver grayish in color and the flavor is earthy and buttery.*

Hackleback: *American hackleback caviar comes from the shovelnose sturgeon fish from the Central United States. The eggs are glistening black eggs, and the flavor is nutty and buttery.*

Serving Caviar

To serve caviar, you can place the cans of caviar on ice or put the caviar in small glass bowls to set on top of the ice. Caviar has a chemical reaction with any kind of metal that alters the flavor and causes the eggs to break down quickly. To serve, use a mother of pearl spoon or a plastic spoon. Both of these are not reactive and allow the full flavor of the caviar to remain intact. When you serve fine caviar, you should eat it within two hours of opening the can. The quality deteriorates quickly with the exposure to air.

IF MEMORY SERVES

Once in my life I thought I had the epitome of a New Year's Eve party. Of course, it was when I was 21 years old and knew everything. This party lives in my memory as my favorite New Year's Eve party ever. I tied the invitations around the necks of champagne bottles and hand–delivered them. The instructions explained that the bottle was the guest's admission ticket. As the guests arrived, we put each of the bottles into a tub of ice. At midnight, everyone went into the backyard and simultaneously opened the bottles. It was a spectacular display of flying corks and spraying champagne. What fun! My mother had such fun that she stayed up and danced for the next two hours with all my friends.

HOW TO OPEN A CHAMPAGNE BOTTLE

Early in my career a dear friend taught me the "proper" way to open champagne.It never fails:

1. *Point the top of the bottle away from you and anyone else in the room and tilt it about 45–50 degrees.*

2. *Remove the foil cover and the wire cap.*

3. *Place a linen napkin (or a light-weight towel) over the top of the bottle.*

4. *Hold the neck of the bottle in your left hand and the base of the bottle with your right hand.*

5. *Holding the cork in place with your left hand, gently turn the bottle toward your body—or counterclockwise—with your right hand until the cork gently releases.*

MAKING ICE BLOCKS

My favorite part of this whole menu is the handcrafted ice blocks designed to serve the caviar and keep it cold for long periods of time. To make ice blocks, take empty cardboard milk cartons and cut the tops off. (Of course, wash them out first.) Fill them with different levels of distilled water. (Distilled water freezes clearer then other waters.) Place them in the freezer for 6–8 hours or overnight. Peel the cartons away, and you will have blocks for serving. If you want to make indentions in the ice to hold a small bowl, about 3 to 4 hours into freezing process, place a small bowl on top of partially frozen water. It should be frozen enough for the bowl to stay on top but not too frozen.

You can freeze vodka bottles this way, too. First of all, choose pretty bottles. Place them inside the cartons and fill with distilled water. Add colorful flowers, herbs and fruits for texture and color if you desire. Experiment with different colors of vodka bottles.

WINE AND SPARKLING WINE BOTTLE SIZES

Miniature	*3.4 ounces*	
Split	*6.3 ounces*	
Half Bottle	*12.7 ounces*	
Bottle 750 ml	*25.4 ounces*	
One Liter	*33.8 ounces*	
Magnum	*50.7 ounces*	*2 Bottles*
Double Magnum	*101.5 ounces*	*4 Bottles*
Jeroboam	*152.2 ounces*	*6 Bottles*
Methuselah/Imperial	*202.9 Ounces*	*8 Bottles*
Salmanazar	*304.4 ounces*	*12 bottles*
Balthazar	*405.8 ounces*	*16 bottles*
Nebuchadnezzar	*507.3 ounces*	*20 bottles*

ELIZABETH STONE AN INVITATION TO ENTERTAIN

The Sweeter Side

Finally, the pièce de résistance. Here are suggestions focused only on one taste bud, one food group, and the one outstanding essence of almost any meal… the dessert. Even if you claim you are not a dessert lover, you have to admit that an outstanding dessert that completes your palate is a wonderful finish to a great meal. My theory in entertaining is start high and finish high. Leave them with something they'll remember.

I have created many "Dessert Only" events for clients. What a great way to entertain inexpensively. As with all entertaining, the idea is to have fun and be creative. Prepare what you enjoy to cook, and buy or outsource the rest. As I tell my staff each and every day, recognize and manage your weaknesses and work hard to improve your strengths. It is a much better and more peaceful use of your time and energy.

Enjoy and Be Sweet!

Dark and White Chocolate Mousse in Champagne Flutes

Toasted Coconut Meringue Tartlets

Dark Chocolate Cheesecake Tarts with Chocolate Crust
and Chocolate Ganache Topping

White Wine poached Pears
filled with Mascarpone Mousse

Chocolate Wafer Cookies dipped in White Chocolate

Almond Macaroons dusted with Powdered Sugar

Triple Chocolate Decadence Cake

Black and White Candies:
Snow Drops
M&Ms
Chocolate Chips
Mini Marshmallows
Chocolate Covered Almonds
Chocolate Covered Cherries

Blanc de Blanc Champagne

Chocolate Martinis

After Dinner Cordials

Post Phantom

DESSERT PARTY

Before this event, all the guests had been to a showing of Phantom of the Opera. The invitation requested everyone arrive in black and white. The waiters were appropriately adorned in tuxedo with tails and phantom masks. It's not necessary to go to this extreme, but it certainly was fun for the guests to be greeted at the door with multiple phantoms lined up offering glasses of champagne and port. A themed event like this should be fun, and not stuffy in the least. I think parties like this are an opportunity to be a little—or really—out of the box.

Following the theme, the desserts, the flowers, the

serving pieces and the décor were all black and white. Most of the dark and white chocolate delicacies were displayed on a tiered stand sitting on a round table covered with a black satin cloth adorned with wide stripes of white satin ribbon. We made the stand with various sizes of wooden table tops from the local home improvement store and thin plywood wrapped to create round cylinder risers between the layers. The entire stand was painted white and wrapped with black satin ribbons around the table edges adhered with double stick tape. This incredible creation was the work of Rebekah Johnson of Bergner Johnson Design.

LET THEM EAT CAKE

Early in my career, I was very naïve. I just wanted to do anything for anybody. Age and wisdom have taught me to do what I do best and stick to it. Here's how I learned to leave cakes to the cake professionals. Don't think I'm discouraging you from making cakes. Rather, I'm admitting a weakness. I've learned if I don't do it well, I turn it over to someone who does.

About 20 years ago, in my first commercial kitchen in a very old small house, I worked with my friends and anyone who would put up with me making whatever anyone wanted. One day a client called and asked me to make her a birthday cake. It was August, and if you don't live in Houston you need to know it was hot and humid. In August, the average temperature is 98 degrees and 90% plus in humidity. Being overly desirous of business because most of my clients had gone to Colorado, I agreed to take on the birthday cake. Really, how hard could it be? I had made cakes before. This time, I had to make the cake portion three times. The first two did not live up to my expectations. I trimmed the pieces to make them perfectly flat and round. I was so proud of myself at this moment. Then came the icing…I looked up the perfect icing recipe from Martha Stewart. How could it go wrong? You name the ways. At this point I was four hours into this one cake. I finished it and was most proud of my creation. I called the client to tell her I was en route with the cake. I carefully placed it in the car and off I went. As I arrived at the client's house, all of the icing slid off the cake. My creation had melted into a buttery mess. So now I don't make cakes.

On only one other occasion, I succumbed to another client's request to make and deliver a cake to a friend of hers. By this time, I had hired a cook who did have experience with cakes. I had a great sense of confidence that no icing would slide this time. I negotiated to have it delivered to the client by one of my staff. This young lady lived in the nearby neighborhood and was sure that she knew exactly where the house was located. She successfully delivered the cake to an exuberant honoree who graciously accepted the cake. Whew—we did it. The cake was delivered. One hour later the client called and asked, "Where is the cake?" You must imagine the quizzical look on my face. Well apparently, the young lady had delivered the cake to a home with the same house number one block north on the wrong street. They, too, were celebrating a birthday and thought that someone had sent them an anonymous cake. They had already cut and eaten it.

Needless to say, that was the last cake made in my kitchen. Cakes are not us.

DIFFERENT TYPES OF CHOCOLATE

Chocolate is the product of a refining process made from the seed of the tropical Theobroma cacao tree. The seeds of the cacao tree have an intense bitter taste and must be fermented to develop the flavor. After fermentation, the beans are dried, roasted and the shell is removed. They are ground and the resulting products are cocoa butter and chocolate liquor, otherwise known as ground roasted cocoa beans. The type of chocolate is determined by the amounts of cocoa butter and chocolate liquor in the product.

Cocoa powder: *This is the unsweetened powder of the cacao bean and has little or no cocoa butter. This powder has an intense chocolate taste.*

Unsweetened chocolate: *This is pure chocolate liquor, composed solely of ground cocoa beans. It is also known as Bitter or Baking chocolate. Unsweetened chocolate is made to be used in cooking. Unsweetened chocolate is the base ingredient in all other forms of chocolate, except white chocolate.*

Dark chocolate: *Dark chocolate contains chocolate liquor with sugar and cocoa butter added. The cocoa content of dark chocolate bars can range from 30% to 80%. Bittersweet chocolate and semi-sweet chocolate also fall into the "dark chocolate" category.*

Bittersweet chocolate: *This chocolate must contain at least 50% chocolate liquor and 35% cocoa solids with sugar added.*

Semi-sweet chocolate: *Semi-sweet chocolate contains at least 35% cocoa solids, and is generally sweeter than bittersweet.*

Milk chocolate: *In addition to containing cocoa butter and chocolate liquor, milk chocolate contains either condensed milk or dry milk solids. Milk chocolate must contain at least 10% chocolate liquor and 12% milk solids.*

White chocolate: *White chocolate gets its name from the cocoa butter it contains, but does not contain chocolate liquor or any other cocoa products.*

MAKE A CARNATION BALL

To make the carnation ball, begin with a large Oasis ball that you can purchase from most craft or floral supply stores. You will need approximately 50 large carnations for a ball that is approximately 8"-10" in diameter. Carnations are very resilient flowers and do not damage easily; thus they work well for this project. Other flowers will work but the more delicate the flower, the more difficult the project. Soak the Oasis ball in water. While the ball is soaking, cut the stem off each of the flowers just under the head. Begin in the center of the ball and work outwards. Attach each flower to the ball using a long straight pin placed in the center of each flower. When you have finished, sprinkle the ball with water and allow to drain overnight into a pan. Your carnation ball will be ready to display the next day. The ball will last approximately 3-4 days. Check, remove and replace flowers as they die.

MENU

Crème Brulee with Caramelized Strawberries

Iced Lemon Mousse with Pistachios,
Lavender Anglaise and Raspberries

Dark Chocolate Pot de Crème
with Espresso Cream

Crêpes Suzette

Bananas Foster

Vanilla Ice Cream

Port Wine and Muscato

French

PATISSERIE

The French are known for delicious desserts. The five basic ingredients for almost every French dessert are flour, sugar, eggs, butter and cream. Of course, fruits, herbs, brandy and other flavors are often added, but these basic five will get you through the basics of most desserts that are French in origin.

A client asked me to create this event for a late night gathering after the debut of the ballet, Giselle. The theme was French country kitchen and we chose classic French desserts, French pottery and simple country French style flowers. We wanted to provide a casual gathering after a fabulous ballet with delectable desserts and dessert wines.

I love the food on this menu—all things French and all things decadent. What could be wrong with Bananas Foster, Crepes Suzettes, Chocolate Pot de Crème, Crème Brulee and Cold Lemon Souffle? Of these desserts, two of them have great memories for me: one of them fond and the other, well, a nightmare.

Crepes Suzettes were my father's favorite dessert. Whenever and wherever we went to a nice meal, he always ordered Crepes Suzette. Being a self taught cook, who specialized in breakfast and steaks, he always had an added note for the chef cooking the crepes. Dad was sure that he knew the exact proportion of sugar to butter to liquor. He always thought there was not enough butter. Frustrated that the table chefs would not listen to his advice, he began creating these delicacies at home. It was an all-afternoon-and-multiple-bowl,-dish-and pan experience. Of course, Mom loved the final result but the dishes were always piled high in the sink. Hours and hours of making delicate crepes one by one and then finally at the end of the meal, creating the perfect sauce of butter and more butter, sugar and a little fresh squeezed orange juice. Then, for the finale, the flame. Except, once the liquor was poured in, there was no flame. What happened! Were they right in the restaurants? Their recipe was the one that created the big dramatic flame at the table. Well, not really. What we learned, after multiple tries, is that you get the mixture of the butter, sugar and juice *very hot* before adding the alcohol. Once you add the alcohol into the bubbling syrup, the mixture will quickly catch on fire and burn off the alcohol, leaving the intoxicating aroma and

luscious flavor. Even with no flame from time to time, Dad's crepes still tasted great.

On the other hand, the Iced Lemon Soufflé probably represents my most traumatic catering story. It was a Saturday in December very early in my career. I thought I could conquer the world and do anything related to food. Boy, did I get a harsh case of reality on this cold winter night. Back then, two parties at the same time on the same night was a huge challenge. Now we average six to eight on one evening in December. Both parties had departed The Stone Kitchen. My chef and I were exhausted. The Iced Lemon Soufflés, 50 of them, had taken Miss Judy over six hours to prepare. They were the last item to be loaded on the truck. They were very delicate and needed to be handled with care. Upon arrival at the client's, the event captain opened the back door of the van. The contents had shifted during transport. As the doors opened, the case of red wine leaped out followed by all fifty Lemon Soufflés. Yes, can you see it: the floor of the client's garage covered with red wine and glass-soaked Lemon soufflé. The captain was panicked and called me at the kitchen. I thought I was going to have a nervous breakdown. Fortunately, my chef had gotten more sleep than I and started calling all the fine restaurants in Houston to see who had fifty servings of one dessert. We were able to find a restaurant with enough dessert and the client, thankfully, was very understanding. Lesson learned. Never sell delicate and difficult desserts for a lot of people and never never put the dessert on top of the boxes of wine. The vision of red wine lemon soufflé will live in my mind forever.

FLAMING DESSERT TRICKS

If you like to put on a show for your guests, an easy, effective way to impress them is to serve a flaming dessert. Most flaming desserts start with a butter and sugar sauce to which a flavor or fruit is added. After those items cook and the flavors blend, it's show time! Make sure that your sauce has a substantial amount of sugar—this will help your flame. Let the sauce cook and come to a boil. Have a bottle of whatever alcohol you want to use to flame your dessert. Depending on the ingredients of my sauce, I like to use Bacardi White Rum, Brandy or Jack Daniels. Melt the butter and the sugar in a skillet. Add the fruit, or whatever flavor you want to add. Bring the mixture to a rigorous boil. Add a generous amount of alcohol to the pan (about ½ to one cup). The mixture will bubble and a great deal of steam will rise from the pan. If you pull the skillet slightly off the burner and tilt it slightly to the flame, it will catch on fire. Don't be afraid. The flames will be big at first but will quickly diminish. The flames are created from the alcohol in the liquor. Once this burns for a few seconds, the alcohol will evaporate and the flames will die out. Make sure the lights are off for a really great show. Gently shake the pan or stir with a spoon, and the alcohol will burn off in 30 seconds to one minute. Your flambéed sauce can be served over crepes or vanilla ice cream. Enjoy!

GREAT FOOD MOVIES

Babette's Feast (1987)

Big Night (1996)

Chocolat (2000)

French Kiss (1995)

Julie and Julia (2009)

Last Holiday (2006)

Ratatouille (2007)

Sabrina (1954)

The Cook, the Thief, His Wife and Her Lover (1989)

MENU

Citrus Fusion
Lemon Bars, Blood Orange Anglaise and Toasted Meringue,
Grand Marnier Ice Cream, Lemonicello Reduction and Pistachio Biscotti,
Caramelized Blood Orange Segments and Candied Pistachios

The Chocoholic
Warm Chocolate Molten Cake, Espresso Chocolate Mousse and
Blackberry Cabernet Sorbet, Balsamic Reduction, Fresh Blackberries,
Chocolate Covered Espresso Beans, Toasted Salted Hazelnuts and
White and Dark Chocolate Shards

Raspberry Rose Vacherin
Raspberry Sorbet and Rose with Greek Yogurt Mousse
with Raspberries, Candied Orange Peel and Edible Rose Petals,
Raspberry Orange Rose Reduction, and Rose Meringue Cookies

Quattro Apple
Warm Granny Smith Apple Galette, Sauterne Poached McIntosh Apples,
Calvados Cream Caramel Sauce and Apple Basil Ginger Granita
Cinnamon Sugar Cookies

Cherry Peach Leaning Napoleon
Caramelized Peaches topped with Cherry Crème Brulee
Fresh Rainier and Bing Cherry Halves with a Peach Lavender Reduction
Peach Sorbet, Almond Lace Cookie

The Essence of Cream
Crème Caramel drizzled with a smooth Caramel Sauce and Fleur de Sel,
Crème Brulee with a brown Sugar Crust and Buttermilk Panna Cotta
topped with whipped Crème Fraiche,
finished with a Mango Pomegranate Coulis, Kiwi and
Pomegranate Seed Confetti with a Crispy Toile

Award Winning

DESSERTS

I've presented you with parties and meals for all kinds of occasions. It is fitting to leave you with the traditional end for the finest meal: a selection of over-the-top, award-winning desserts. If you're always up for a cooking challenge and you want to push beyond traditional food boundaries, these sweets are for you.

The desserts here have been inspired by many chefs who have a tremendous ability to fuse flavors and textures into something absolutely incredible. The dessert experience awes me; it challenges me to push the boundaries and create culinary experiences that delight and please the palates of others.

Each of these desserts is somewhat—if not very—complicated. Please refine them or add to them as you desire. When creating these desserts, my main goal was to touch all the senses. It must be beautiful. It must emit an aroma that begs you to eat it. It must have at least three to four texture or temperature components. And last, but most important, it must touch your tongue and make you say "I can't get enough of this."

Two of these desserts secured me "Dessert Chef of the Year" awards for two consecutive years. It started one day when a client suggested that I enter The Food and Wine Week Dessert competition because her company was the sponsor. I laughed and told her I'm not a dessert chef. They had enough competitors in the Savory Food section and they needed more contestants for dessert. OK, I said as my arm was twisted. What else would I say to this wonderful client?

Four days before the event, I realized that I had not created my dessert. To a caterer, four days is an eternity, but to most people, it seemed that I had lost my mind. And that might be the case. I read all the dessert cookbooks that I owned and created the most outrageous, complicated dessert ever. What was I thinking? Oh, one more thing: the competition demanded that entrants create 600- 2 oz servings of their dessert. There's nothing like a good challenge to put the team to a test! I always chalk it up to team building.

My first dessert competition entry was the Raspberry Rose Vacherin, listed below. I took my entire management team to the competition, and it took all five of us three hours to assemble the dessert. At the end of the evening, they proclaimed us the winner. We were presented with a check for $1000 and a Waterford trophy. At that moment, it all seemed worth it.

I decided to enter a second time to "Uphold my Title." This time the dessert was a little less complicated, but not much. The Peach Cherry Napoleon brought in the prize again. I am blessed to have an incredible group of people that work with me and put up with my outlandish ideas. My team is dear to me. I wouldn't be anywhere without them. They are the real sweets in my life, and it's their willingness to go with me, on sometimes bizarre culinary adventures, that has allowed me to learn so many delightful ways that food can be prepared and presented.

CHERRIES

Some people think cherries are the pits, and they're afraid to deal with them. It's easy to remove the pit from ripe cherries—just cut the cherry in half and remove the pit with a small spoon. Or, you can cut down the center with a small knife until you hit the pit. Take the cherry, open it with your finger and use your thumb to remove the seed. The third alternative is to buy a neat gadget called a cherry pitter. It is easy to use and so much fun.

Bing Cherries: This cherry has red skin and flesh. The pit is usually small and the flesh is firm and juicy. When these are dark red or burgundy they are ripe and ready to eat. They are slightly soft but not mushy. If they're still bright red and firm, they are not ripe yet. The bing cherries have a strong burst of cherry flavor, and are slightly tart and sweet at the same time.

Ranier Cherries: These cherries are a yellow golden color with patches of bright pink. Their color doesn't change as much with ripeness, but they will soften a little as they ripen and release their natural sweetness. They are generally sweeter than the red cherries, with a more subtle flavor. These cherries were developed in 1952 by crossing the Bing with the Van cultivar.

MAKING MERINGUE

Don't be afraid of meringue. It is simply a mixture of egg whites and sugar. How hard can that be? The real trick to making great meringue is how you beat the egg whites. Egg whites can be very finicky. Make sure that your bowl and beaters are both well dried. Separate the egg yolks from the egg whites. Carefully separate the eggs making sure that no yellow gets into the whites. This will ruin the meringue. The whites will not whip. Allow the whites to sit for 30 minutes and come to room temperature. The egg whites will grow six to eight times their volume once they are beaten. Be sure to use a large bowl. When beating the whites, they will first get frothy, then they will form soft peaks. (When you remove the beaters from the whites, the whites form peaks that hold but are not stiff.) Then add your sugar and beat until the sugar is completely dissolved. You will have perfect meringue every time.

Recipes

HOW TO TOAST NUTS, SEEDS OR COCONUT

Here are three ways to toast nuts, seeds or coconut:

Stove Top: *In a heavy bottomed skillet, spread your nuts out in an even layer and heat them over medium heat while shaking often. Keep stirring or shaking for about five minutes, or until nuts are fragrant and browned. Nuts toasted using the stove top method will not be uniformly browned, but more mottled in appearance. Do not try to toast different kinds of nuts at the same time. Different nuts will toast at different rates.*

Stove Top (with oil/butter): *If you want to toast on the stove-top, but also want that uniformly browned look, you can add a scant teaspoon of oil or butter to the pan and shake it to cover your nuts. This will result in a more evenly toasted nut – but a slightly oilier final product.*

Oven: *You can also toast any kind of nut in a hot oven. Preheat an oven to 350-425 degrees. Place your nuts on a baking sheet and bake for 5-10 minutes. Watch the nuts carefully and shake occasionally. They are done when golden and fragrant. Oven toasted nuts yield the best flavor in my opinion .*

DAIRY: CREAM, MILK AND BUTTER

Nonfat Milk	*Less than .25% milk fat*
2% Milk	*2% milk fat*
Whole Milk	*3.5 % milk fat*
Half & Half	*10% milk fat*
Light Cream	*18% milk fat*
Whipping Cream	*34% milk fat*
Heavy Cream	*36% milk fat*
Butter	*>80% milk fat*

* Heavy Cream substitution (not whipping cream):
⅓ cup butter & ⅔ cup whole milk

MEASUREMENT CONVERSIONS

Pinch	=	*¹⁄₁₆ Teaspoon*
3 Teaspoons	=	*1 Tablespoon*
16 Tablespoons	=	*1 Cup*
2 Cups	=	*1 Pint*
4 Cups	=	*1 Quart*
4 Quarts	=	*1 Gallon*
1 Gallon	=	*128 Fluid Ounces or 4 Quarts or 8 Pints or 16 Cups*
2 Tablespoons	=	*1 Fluid Ounce*

SALTS

What's the fuss about all these salts? Which salt should you use in your grinder?

Iodized Salt: *the most commonly used salt, table salt. It's granulated and has Iodine added.*

Kosher Salt: *a crystal salt that is course in texture and has no additives. It will draw liquid from meats. This salt is easy to cook with, as it is more forgiving than other salts and allows you to not over-salt as easily. Kosher salt brings out the natural flavors in food without adding too much of that salty taste.*

Sea Salt: *made from evaporated seawater, and has a thin, flaky texture. Sea salts have a unique flavor and taste. Each one is slightly different. I love to use this type of salt for finishing, or after the dish or item is cooked to put on at the end and add an additional layer of flavor.*

French Sea Salts: *also from evaporated seawater, these salts are generally unrefined and retain some of the natural minerals from the water.*

Gray Salt (sel gris): *comes from the clay lining of the French sea basins.*

Fleur de Sel (flower of salt): *from Gray Salt, but lighter in color*

Pink Salt: *Himalayan Pink Salt is a pure, hand-mined salt that is derived from ancient sea salt deposits, and it is believed to be the purest form of salt available. The high mineral crystals range in color from sheer white, varying shades of pink, to deep reds, the result of high mineral and iron content. The newest hottest cooking technique is to actually cook on a Pink Salt Plate. The Himalayan Salt Slabs or plates have the ability to be cooled to 0 degrees or heated to 500 degrees and then hold their temperature for a while. I have used them in catering to serve sushi on as it keeps everything very cold and fresh and also I have actually had a station at an event where we seared raw beef on the plates and they tasted great.*

KITCHEN BASIC SPICES

It's important to keep the basic ingredients around, but there's no need for 450 different spices. If you don't use them up frequently, their flavor will fade and you'll be forced to buy new ones again when you actually need them. Here are a few that I use regularly and always have on hand:

Salt: *Plain iodized salt is the most basic of "basic" ingredients to have.*

Fancy Salt: *Look for a kosher salt or fleur de sel.*

Seasoned Salt: *My favorite kind of seasoned salt is Jane's Mixed up Krazy Salt. Lawry's Seasoned Salt is also great.*

Black Pepper: *Look for black pepper that is cracked and in a table grinder.*

White Pepper: *White pepper comes from the same plant as black pepper, but it ripens longer and has a slightly different taste.*

Beau Monde: *This spice mix from Spice Islands is the perfect blend of celery, onion and salt. I love this on poultry and meats.*

Fines Herbs/Italian Herbs: *Herbs dress up any dish from a sandwich to pasta. There are many varieties, so pick two or three to keep around for instant gratification.*

KNIVES

If you like to cook, selecting a knife that you like to work with is very important, and will make the difference in a positive and negative cooking experience. A good knife does not have to be expensive but there are a few things that you should consider. First, and most important, make sure it feels good in your hands. There are all sorts of blades for all sorts of uses. I prefer to work with a 8" chef's knife for most of my cutting. When deciding to buy a knife, make sure that you choose one with a full tang,—the blade's steel must run through the handle of the knife. A full tang adds strength, weight and balance to a knife. Keep your knives sharp. A sharp knife is safer than a dull knife. When using a dull knife you have to add additional pressure to cut and the knife will tend to slip off the food and cut you. Working with a sharp knife requires little force; it's easier to control and it cuts where intended.

FOOD SAFETY

Chicken: *We want to think that nothing we buy at the grocery store would have bacteria, but careful handling of raw chicken is extremely important. It is very common for raw chicken to have the bacteria salmonella. Be careful to clean everything—including your hands—very well after you work with raw chicken. Don't let greens or other items you are washing go on the same counter or in the sink where chicken has been until you've washed the surface with soap. Salmonella is easily killed when you cook chicken at high enough temperatures. Your chicken should never be pink inside unless you are smoking it. When you poke it with a fork or cut it slightly with a knife, the juices should be clear with no pink or red color. Until that point, the chicken has not cooked long enough or reached a temperature high enough to kill the bacteria.*

AFTER DINNER CORDIALS

Aperitifs are an alcoholic beverage taken before a meal to cleanse your palette and whet your appetite. After dinner cordials are referred to as digestifs, which are consumed after dinner and are intended to aid in the digestion process, as the name suggests. There are over a hundred liquers or cordials (a stimulating drink). A gracious host or hostess might offer a selection of three to five. Be sure to include at least one sweet and one non sweet. I might suggest a Grappa, a Cognac, Grand Marnier, Kahlua, Bailey's Irish Cream, and maybe Lemoncello.

Grappa: *Brandy distilled with grape pomace usually from Italy*

Cognac: *Brandy distilled from white wine of the Cognac region of France*

Grand Marnier: *A French cognac based liqueur with flavors of orange, spice and vanilla*

Bailey's Irish Cream: *toffee flavored creamy brandy*

Lemoncello: *Sweetened vodka flavored with lemons*

It is not a requirement to serve after dinner cordials, but if you move from the dining table to the living room to sip on coffee, it is nice to offer your guests a small amount of a cordial.

SEGMENTING CITRUS

Cut the top and bottom off the fruit, deep enough to remove all skin. Peel the rind off the segments. Using a small sharp paring knife, cut around the citrus to completely remove all skin, cell pith (the white part) and outer casing from the segments. Hold the fruit in one hand, and with a sharp knife carefully cut in between each casing and remove the segments.

RICING AN EGG

Hard boil an egg and remove the shell. Press the entire egg through a fine sieve.

Cook with Love, Not Fear

Are you ready to cook for your next party? Here's the best advice I can give you: Cook from your heart. Whether you have always loved to cook or you've been afraid of the room in your house that is called the kitchen, you can create wonderful and exciting food and enjoy the journey.

First, get comfortable with your kitchen. The fear of cooking usually evolves from awkward moments with a knife or a pot of boiling water or—worse—from trying to create perfection. Don't dismay, we all have those moments. Remember, cooking is an art and not a science. If you have the desire, you can cook. If you're really not interested, just eat and enjoy.

Don't worry about your gear. Having the "best" knife or pan has nothing to do with the success of your culinary endeavors. Find a knife that you're comfortable with that feels good in your hand. Some knives cost twenty dollars, and others two hundred. The price doesn't dictate the quality of the meal that you are preparing. My favorite knives are an 8" chef's knife and a paring knife. The 8" knife is long enough to do most jobs, yet short enough to feel comfortable and manageable. The paring knife is great for peeling vegetables and doing small cutting jobs. Look at specialty kitchen stores and commercial kitchen stores: Just because it costs more does not mean it will cook better or cut better. I paid only twenty-five dollars for my favorite knife.

To deal with the "whatevers" and the "what ifs," make sure that you keep butter and cream in your refrigerator. I can fix anything with butter and cream. Believe me when I say that, this is my motto. If my catering staff show up to an event without it, they might as well go back to the kitchen. Extra butter and cream are a standard part of our pack out for each event. Butter and cream have saved me from many "what ifs" in my career. From a dry finger sandwich to an overcooked piece of fish; from a broken sauce to not enough soup to fill the last bowl; from dry rolls to over-salted pasta, cream and butter can fix—and has fixed—almost everything.

And always remember: An outstanding meal is a

wonderful experience, but if the food doesn't quite turn out like you imagined, just keep going. The guests will only remember the "not so great" food if you mention it. Never apologize for a cooking mistake. So, you burned the meat and the vegetables were soggy. Pour your guests a fresh glass of wine and tell them a funny story. The way you make them feel welcome and comfortable is what they will remember.

Enjoy every aspect of the meal: thinking about it, preparing it, sharing it and then remembering it. Hospitality is the heart and soul of entertaining, so make sure that you infuse everything that you serve with love for those who will receive it.

Bon Appetit!

Baked Brie with Port-Poached Figs and Crisp Bacon

Serves 8

8 oz	brie (1 small round)
1 pkg	frozen puff pastry sheets (2 sheets)
½ cup	dried black mission figs
½ cup	Port wine
4 slices	bacon, fried crisp and chopped
1	egg

Preheat oven to 425 degrees. Remove puff pastry sheets from package and thaw until easily able to unfold. Place figs in a medium saucepan, cover with Port wine, and bring to a boil. Remove from the heat, drain, and cut the figs into small pieces. This process softens the figs and releases the flavors. Lay out one sheet of puff pastry on the counter. Place brie in the middle of the sheet. Top brie with the chopped figs and crumbled bacon. In a small bowl, beat 1 egg with 1 tablespoon of water. Fold pastry around brie and using a pastry brush, brush egg wash on all of the parts of the pastry that will touch another part of the pastry. The egg wash helps make the pastry hold together well. Brush the pastry on the outside of the entire brie. Place on baking sheet with the seam side down. Unfold another puff pastry sheet, and using a knife or cookie cutter, cut out a decorative piece to put on top of the brie. Brush the piece with egg wash and place on top of brie round. Bake for 20 minutes or until pastry is golden brown. Serve with French bread and seasonal fruits.

Banana, Fig and Walnut Bread Sandwiches with Cream Cheese

Serves 8

2½ cups	flour
1 tsp	baking soda
1 tsp	cinnamon
½ tsp	salt
¼ cup	butter (½ stick), softened
1 cup	sugar
2 lg	eggs
3 lg	ripe bananas, peeled and mashed
5 Tbsp	buttermilk
½ cup	walnuts pieces
½ cup	dried black mission figs, cut into small pieces

Sandwich Filling:

8 oz	cream cheese, softened

Bread:

Preheat the oven to 350 degrees. Prepare a loaf pan by greasing it generously with butter. In a medium mixing bowl, mix together the flour, baking soda, cinnamon and salt. In another bowl, beat with an electric mixer the butter and sugar until light and fluffy. Add the eggs one at a time and stir in the bananas and buttermilk. Gradually add the flour mix to the bananas and buttermilk mix. Fold in the walnuts and figs. Pour into prepared loaf pan. Bake until an inserted toothpick comes out with just a few crumbs on it, about 45 minutes-1 hour. Allow to cool completely before slicing. Bread can be made the day ahead and stored at room temperature wrapped in foil.

Sandwich Assembly:

Once cooled, slice the bread into thin slices. Spread each slice with softened cream cheese and top with another slice. Cut the sandwiches into halves. Place sandwiches on a platter and refrigerate until ready to serve. You may store these overnight in an airtight container in the refrigerator.

Basic Buttermilk Biscuit Recipe

Yields 30 Biscuits

4 cups	flour
2 Tbsp	sugar
2 Tbsp	baking powder
1 tsp	baking soda
1 tsp	salt
¾ lb	butter, chilled and cut into small pieces
2 cups	cold buttermilk

Preheat oven to 400 degrees. Combine flour, sugar, baking powder, baking soda and salt in a food processor and blend. Add butter using the on/off switch to pulse the batter to a fine meal consistency; do not over mix. Transfer batter to a large bowl. Slowly add buttermilk into the batter until it becomes a dough (you may not need to add all of the buttermilk). Put the dough onto a floured surface and knead gently until well combined (about 10 turns). Pat out the dough until it is about ¾-1 inch thick. Cut the biscuits out with a 2-2½ inch round cookie cutter. Pull together all remaining scraps and pat them out into ¾ inch thickness and cut additional biscuits. Transfer biscuits to 9 inch round pan, sprayed well with food release or Pam. Each pan should have 12 biscuits, 9 around the perimeter and 3 in the middle. Bake for 12-15 minutes or until golden brown.

BLACK PEPPER CHEDDAR BISCUITS

Yields 30 Biscuits

1 Tbsp	black pepper
2 cups	extra sharp cheddar cheese, grated

Follow the same instruction as the Basic Buttermilk Biscuits. Add the black pepper in with the salt. After transferring the batter into a bowl and before adding buttermilk, fold the cheese into the mixture.

GOAT CHEESE AND TARRAGON BISCUITS

Yields 30 biscuits

1 tsp	dried tarragon
1 cup	goat cheese, crumbled

Follow the same instruction as the Basic Buttermilk Biscuits. Add the dried tarragon with the salt. After transferring the batter into a bowl and before adding buttermilk, fold the cheese into the mixture.

WHITE CHEDDAR AND CHIVE BISCUITS

Yields 30 biscuits

1 Tbsp	chives, minced
2 cups	white cheddar cheese, grated

Follow the same instruction as the Basic Buttermilk Biscuits. Add the chives with the salt. After transferring the batter into a bowl and before adding buttermilk, fold the cheese into the mixture.

TOASTED CHIVE BISCUITS

Yields 30 biscuits

1 cup	melted butter

Follow the instructions for the White Cheddar and Chive Biscuits but do not add the cheese. Once the biscuits are baked and cooled, cut them in half and brush heavily with the melted butter. Toast in a 300 degree oven for 10-15 minutes, until golden brown.

Basic Cream Scones
Yields 24 Scones

2 cups	flour
1 Tbsp	baking powder
¼ cup	sugar
⅓ cup	butter, cut into pieces
1 cup	heavy cream

Preheat the oven to 375 degrees. Combine the flour, baking powder and sugar in a food processor. Add the butter and pulse until the mixture is crumbly. Remove the mixture from the food processor and place in a bowl. Stir the heavy cream into the mixture and keep stirring until the mixture is moistened. Knead the mixture on a lightly floured surface about 5-6 times. Roll to a ½ inch thickness and cut with a round cookie cutter. Place 2 inches apart on a greased baking sheet or a baking sheet lined with parchment paper. Bake for 15-20 minutes, or until lightly browned on top.

BACON SCONES
Yields 24 Scones

½ cup	crumbled bacon (approximately 8 slices of bacon)
½ tsp	salt
¼ tsp	black pepper

Follow the same instructions as for the Basic Cream Scones. Do not add the sugar. Add the salt, pepper and crumbled bacon when adding the heavy cream.

ORANGE SCONES WITH ORANGE BUTTER
Yields 24 scones

3 Tbsp	orange zest

Follow the same instructions as for the Basic Cream Scones. Add orange zest when adding the heavy cream.

Orange Butter:
Yields 1 cup

¾ cup	butter (or 1½ sticks), softened
¼ cup	orange marmalade

In a small mixing bowl, mix together butter and marmalade, using a fork. Blend well. Refrigerate until ready to serve.

DRIED CHERRY, CRANBERRY, AND CURRANT SCONES WITH CLOTTED CREAM
Yields 24 scones

¼ cup	dried cherries
¼ cup	dried cranberries
⅛ cup	dried currants
2 cups	clotted cream (can be purchased at store)

Follow the same instructions as for the Basic Cream Scones. Add dried fruits when adding the heavy cream. Served with clotted cream.

Buttered Toast Points
Yields 40 Toast Points

1 loaf	thin white bread (I love Pepperidge Farm Thin White)
1 cup	butter (or 2 sticks), softened

Preheat oven to 300 degrees. Trim the crust from the bread. Cut the bread in half on the diagonal and then cut each triangle in half again. Spread each piece of bread generously with butter. Toast in the oven for 10-15 minutes until lightly browned and crispy. Cool completely. Store the toast points for up to two weeks in air tight containers.

Cornbread Muffins, Griddled

Yields 20 mini muffins

1½ cups	yellow corn meal
1 cup	all-purpose flour, sifted
⅓ cup	sugar
1 Tbsp	baking powder
1¼ tsp	salt
1½ cups	milk
¾ cup	butter (or 1½ sticks), melted and cooled
2	eggs, slightly beaten
½ cup	butter, melted

Preheat the oven to 400 degrees. Spray mini muffin pans with food release spray or Pam. Mix the cornmeal, flour, sugar, baking powder and salt in a large mixing bowl. In another bowl, mix together the milk, cooled melted butter and eggs. Whisk until blended. Slowly add the milk mixture to the cornmeal mixture until well incorporated. Do not over beat. Spoon mixture into prepared muffin tins until about ¾ full. Bake for 20-25 minutes. Check to make sure they are done by sticking a toothpick in the middle of the muffin until it comes out clean or with just a few crumbs on it. Remove the muffins from the pan while they are still warm. Drizzle with the additional melted butter.

Crostini

Yields 60 pieces

6	frozen soft bread sticks
1 cup	butter (or 2 sticks), melted

Preheat the oven to 300 degrees. Cut the bread sticks into thin slices approximately ¼ of an inch thick. Place the slices on a baking sheet and use a pastry brush to brush the bread heavily with butter. Toast the bread in the oven for about 15-20 minutes, until crispy and lightly browned. Be careful not to overcook the bread, it can burn easily. If the crostini are not crispy after 15 minutes, return them to the oven and check every 5 minutes. Store the crostini for up to two weeks in an airtight container.

Dinner Crepes (Basic Crepe Batter)

Yields 24 crepes

¾ cup	milk
¾ cup	cold water
3	egg yolks
1½ cups	flour, sifted
5 Tbsp	butter, melted
¼ cup	vegetable oil

Mix all of the ingredients together in an electric blender. Blend for 1 minute at highest speed. Place the batter in the refrigerator for 2-4 hours. While waiting for batter to chill, cut 24 squares of wax paper about 6" x 6" to use for stacking the crepes. When ready to cook crepes, place 1 teaspoon of vegetable oil in a crepe skillet (or small omelet pan) and heat on medium-high heat for 1 minute. Pour a ½ cup of batter into the heated, oiled crepe pan and twirl the pan until the batter looks like a thin pancake. Cook the crepe until it is lightly browned on one side. Gently remove the crepe from the pan using a rubber spatula and place onto a plate. Place a piece of wax paper on top of crepe and continue this process until all the crepes are cooked. Stacking the crepes with wax paper keeps them from sticking to each other and makes for easy storage.

NOTE: If you have never made crepes before, do not despair. It can be a little tricky but it is worth the effort. This is a process that takes a little patience and sometimes a few tries to get it right. If the first couple of crepes do not work, add a little flour to the mixture and try again. You will eventually get the hang of it.

Garlic Accented Tuscan Toast

Serves 8 pieces

1	Italian bread loaf or French baguette
1 cup	olive oil
2 tsp	granulated garlic

Heat stove top griddle or outdoor grill on high. Slice the loaf into ½-¾ inch slices. In a small bowl, mix granulated garlic with olive oil. Brush the oil mixture onto one side of bread. Place bread on grill or griddle olive oil side down. Grill for 1-2 minutes until slightly toasted.

Gingerbread with Brown Sugar Crème Fraîche

Serves 24

½ cup	boiling water
1 cup	dark molasses (not blackstrap)
¼ cup	light corn syrup
1 tsp	baking soda
2 cups	flour
1½ tsp	baking powder
2 tsp	ground ginger
2 tsp	ground cinnamon
¼ tsp	ground cloves
¼ tsp	allspice
⅛ tsp	ground nutmeg
¾ cup	butter
1 cup	dark brown sugar
1 cup	sour cream
3 lg	eggs, beaten

Preheat the oven to 325 degrees. Butter a 13 by 9 inch baking pan and sprinkle with flour. Shake pan so the flour covers all of the parts and shake off excess. In a mixing bowl, whisk together the molasses, light corn syrup and the boiling water until the mixture is smooth. Stir in the baking soda and set aside. In another mixing bowl, sift together flour, baking powder, ginger, cinnamon, cloves, allspice and nutmeg. In another large mixing bowl, beat together the butter and the sugar. Add the sour cream and blend until well mixed. Add the beaten eggs and molasses mixture. Gently, whisk in the flour mixture until just combined. Pour into a baking pan. Tap pan on counter once sharply to remove excess air bubbles. Bake for 40-50 minutes. Remove from oven and allow to cool.

BROWN SUGAR CRÈME FRAÎCHE

Yields 2 cups

1 cup	sour cream
2 Tbsp	brown sugar
1 cup	heavy cream

In a medium mixing bowl, stir together sour cream and brown sugar. In another bowl, beat the heavy cream until stiff peaks form. Fold the whipped cream into the sour cream mixture.

Perfect Pizza Dough

Yields (2) 9 inch pizzas

1 Tbsp	extra virgin olive oil
⅔ cup	luke-warm water (110 degrees)
1 tsp	active dry yeast
2 cups	all-purpose flour
1 tsp	salt

Coat a mixing bowl with olive oil and set aside. Pour the warm water into another small mixing bowl and sprinkle with the yeast. Stir the yeast into water and let sit for about 1 minute. Make sure the yeast is completely dissolved. In a large bowl (or on your clean counter), mix 2 cups flour with the salt. Create a mound with the flour and make a small hole with your fist in the middle of the flour. Pour the yeast and water mixture into the hole. Gently mix the flour with the yeast mixture until completely combined and you have a soft dough. Lightly coat the counter with a little flour. Too much flour will make your dough dry. Knead the dough until the ball of dough becomes smooth and almost elastic. You can pull and punch the dough in order to knead it. This can take up to 8-10 minutes. If you feel that the dough is too dry, add one tablespoon of water. If the dough is very sticky add a little flour. Once you have kneaded the dough place it in a bowl that you have coated with olive oil. Cover the bowl with plastic (or wax paper) and place it in a warm place for about 1-1½ hours. It will double in size. I like to put the dough in my oven before I turn it on. Once the dough has risen, punch the dough down and cut in half. Form each half into a ball. Flatten the dough with your hands (or roll the dough to the desired thickness and size desired using a rolling pin.) Add topping and bake for 10-15 minutes at 400 degrees until crust is slightly crispy and browned.

NOTE: The temperature of the water is the most important part of this recipe because the temperature of the water will activate the yeast. If the water is too cold, the yeast will not activate. If the water is too hot, it will kill the yeast. Use an instant read thermometer to determine the water temperature. The temperature can range from 105 degrees to 115 degrees.

After trying numerous dough recipes, I decided that this one was the most consistent and created a flavorful and crispy crust. Hope you enjoy.

PIZZA BIANCA

Yields (1) 9 inch pizza

1 med	pizza crust (use Perfect Pizza Dough recipe or purchase from store)
2 Tbsp	extra virgin olive oil
¾ cup	shredded mozzarella cheese
½ cup	shredded white cheddar cheese
⅓ cup	shredded manchego cheese
1 tsp	dried italian herbs (or 2 tsp of fresh rosemary)
½ tsp	sea salt

Preheat the oven to 400 degrees. Take the pre-rolled pizza dough and brush with the olive oil. Sprinkle all of the cheeses on top of the dough, and then add the herbs on top of the cheese. Finish with the sea salt. Bake the pizza on a pizza stone (or baking sheet) for 10-15 minutes.

BRIE, PEAR, ARUGULA AND OLIVE OIL WITH BLACK TRUFFLE SALT PIZZA

Yields (1) 9 inch pizza

1 med	pizza crust (use Perfect Pizza Dough recipe or purchase from store)
2 Tbsp	extra virgin olive oil
½ cup	shredded mozzarella cheese
4 oz	Brie cheese, cut into small pieces
1 lg	pear, peeled and sliced thin
1 cup	baby arugula
2 Tbsp	olive oil
½ tsp	black truffle salt

Preheat the oven to 400 degrees. Take the pre-rolled pizza dough and brush with olive oil. Sprinkle the mozzarella and Brie on top of pizza dough. Layer the pear slices over the cheeses. Bake the pizza for 10-15 minutes at 400 degrees on a pizza stone (or baking sheet). Check to make sure dough is done and slightly crispy. Once the pizza is done, remove it from the oven. While the pizza is still hot, toss the arugula with truffle oil and salt. Place the arugula on top of the hot pizza.

CLASSIC PIZZA

Yields (1) 9 inch pizza

1 med	pizza crust (use Perfect pizza dough recipe or purchase from store)
2 Tbsp	tomato sauce
¾ cup	shredded mozzarella cheese
¼ lb	lean ground beef
¼ lb	ground sausage
¼ cup	minced purple onion
¼ cup	diced bell peppers, mixed colors (green, yellow and red)

Preheat the oven to 400 degrees. Take the pre-rolled pizza dough and brush with tomato sauce. Make sure to spread all the way to the edge. Sprinkle the mozzarella cheese on top. Arrange the very small pieces of the raw ground beef and sausage around the pizza. Sprinkle the onions and bell peppers. Bake the pizza on a pizza stone (or baking sheet) for 15 minutes.

SPINACH ALFREDO PIZZA

Yields (1) 9 inch pizza

1 med	pizza crust (use Perfect pizza dough recipe or purchase from store)
2 Tbsp	extra virgin olive oil
¼ cup	butter (or ½ stick)
½ med	onion, chopped
1 clove	garlic, minced
10 oz	frozen chopped spinach, thawed, and squeezed dry
1 cup	heavy cream
½ cup	Parmesan cheese
1 pinch	paprika
½ cup	shredded mozzarella cheese

Preheat the oven to 400 degrees. Take the pre-rolled pizza dough and brush with the olive oil. Spread the spinach Alfredo on the pizza. Sprinkle with mozzarella cheese and bake the pizza on a pizza stone (or baking sheet) for 15 minutes.

Spinach Alfredo:

In a medium heavy bottomed sauce pan, sauté the onion and minced garlic in butter until the onions are translucent. Add the spinach and stir to combine. Add the heavy cream and bring the mixture to a boil, stirring constantly. Add the Parmesan cheese and reduce the heat to simmer and cook for 10-15 minutes. Allow mixture to cool slightly before putting on top of pizza. .

MEDITERRANEAN PIZZA

Yields (1) 9 inch pizza

1 med	chicken breast
1 med	pizza crust (use Perfect pizza dough recipe or purchase from store)
2 Tbsp	olive oil
½ cup	shredded mozzarella cheese
¼ cup	diced sundried tomatoes
½ cup	quartered canned artichoke hearts, drained
¼ cup	sliced Kalamata olives, drained
½ cup	crumbled goat cheese (may substitute cream cheese or Feta cheese)
2 tsp	aged balsamic vinegar
1 Tbsp	extra virgin olive oil

Preheat the oven to 400 degrees. Place the chicken breast in a small baking pan. Season the chicken breast with salt and pepper and roast in the oven for 15-20 minutes. Be sure it is cooked all the way through and that there is no pink meat. While the chicken is still warm, pull it into long strips. Set chicken aside. Take the pre-rolled pizza dough and brush with olive oil. Sprinkle the mozzarella cheese on top of the dough. Layer the sundried tomatoes, artichoke hearts and Kalamata olives on the pizza dough. Bake on a pizza stone (or baking sheet) for 10-15 minutes. Once the pizza is done, remove it from the oven and top with pulled chicken and goat cheese. Return to oven for 5 minutes, or until the cheese is lightly browned and soft. Drizzle with balsamic vinegar and additional olive oil.

Toasted Blueberry Muffins with Honey Butter Glaze

Yields 24 mini muffins

¾ cup	butter (or 1½ sticks)
1 cup	sugar
3 lg	eggs
2½ cups	all-purpose flour, sifted
2 tsp	baking powder
1 tsp	salt
¾ cup	milk
1 tsp	vanilla extract
1¾ cups	fresh blueberries

Preheat the oven to 350 degrees. Prepare muffin tins by lightly greasing with butter. In a large mixing bowl, cream the butter and sugar with an electric mixer until light and fluffy. Add the eggs, one at a time. In a separate mixing bowl, blend together the flour, baking powder and salt. Gently stir the flour mixture into the butter mixture. Then, add the milk and vanilla. Fold in the blueberries. Pour the batter into prepared muffin tins. Bake for 25-30 minutes until golden brown. Remove from the oven and allow to cool for 10 minutes.

Preheat oven to broil. Cut the muffins in half and spread with honey butter. Place the muffin halves on a baking sheet and place under broiler for 1-2 minutes until toasted and golden. Watch closely, they will burn very easily.

NOTE: You may use frozen blueberries if fresh are not available. Be sure to thaw the frozen berries and drain well before putting in the mixture.

HONEY BUTTER GLAZE

Yields 1 cup

¾ cup	butter (or 1½ sticks), softened
¼ cup	honey

In a small mixing bowl, use a fork and stir the honey into the softened butter until well blended.

Yeast Rolls

Yields 4 dozen rolls

2 Tbsp	sugar
2 Tbsp	luke-warm water (110 degrees)
1 pkg	dry yeast
3 lg	eggs
½ cup	sugar
1 cup	luke-warm water (110 degrees)
½ cup	shortening, melted
½ tsp	salt
5 cups	flour
1 cup	butter (or 2 sticks),melted

Preheat the oven to 350 degrees. Brush four 9" cake pans, metal or aluminum, with melted butter. Set aside. In a small bowl, combine the sugar, warm water, and yeast, and stir. Allow the mixture to rest until the yeast has dissolved, about 5-10 minutes. In a large mixing bowl, beat the eggs and sugar. Then, add the luke-warm water, shortening, salt, and flour. Stir in the yeast mixture and mix well, but do not overwork. Form the dough into a ball and leave in the mixing bowl. The dough will be sticky. Place the bowl in a warm place and allow the dough to rise until it reaches the edge of the bowl. Punch down the dough with your fist and place in warm place and allow to rise again.

After the second rise, punch it down again. Remove from mixing bowl and place on a floured surface. Flour a rolling pin and roll the dough out into about ¼ inch thickness. Cut the dough into approximately 2" x 3" squares. Brush each piece with melted butter and fold both ends into the middle and fold in half. Place the folded roll, seam side down into a prepared round cake pan. Place nine rolls around the perimeter of the pan and three in the middle. Allow rolls to rise in the pan before putting in the oven until at least double in size. Brush the tops of the rolls with melted butter and place in the oven and bake for 15-20 minutes, or until golden brown. Remove from oven and brush again with melted butter. Serve hot or top with aluminum and freeze until ready to serve.

NOTE: The temperature of the warm water is the key to success with the recipe. The water can be between 105 and 115 degrees. If the water is too cool, it will not activate the yeast. If the water is too hot, it will kill the yeast. Invest in an instant read kitchen thermometer, available at grocery stores.

HOMEMADE APPLE CINNAMON RAISIN PECAN ROLLS

Serving Size: 12

1	Recipe Yeast Roll Dough
4	granny smith apples, peeled and diced
1 cup	sugar
1 Tbsp	cinnamon
½ cup	pecan pieces, toasted
½ cup	raisins
2 cups	butter (4 sticks),melted

While the dough is rising, in a separate mixing bowl combine the diced apples, sugar, cinnamon, pecan pieces, raisins and butter. Roll the dough out into about ¼ inch thickness. Spread the filling over the dough. Roll the dough into a log and slice into ½ inch pieces. Place in a pan. Allow rolls to rise in pan before baking. There should be 12 rolls per pan. Once risen to at least double in size, bake at 350 degrees for 15 - 20 minutes, or until golden brown. Brush with melted butter once removed from the oven.

OOEY GOOEY ORANGE ROLLS

Serving Size: 12

1	Recipe Yeast Roll Dough
¾ cup	sugar
3 Tbsp	orange zest
2 cups	butter (4 sticks), melted

Icing:

1 cup	sugar
¾ cup	sour cream
3 Tbsp	orange juice
¾ cup	butter (or 1½ sticks)
2 Tbsp	orange zest

While the dough is rising, in a separate mixing bowl combine the sugar, orange zest and butter. Roll the dough out into about ¼ inch thickness. Spread the filling over the dough. Roll the dough into a log and slice into ½ inch pieces. Place in a pan. Allow rolls to rise in pan before baking. There should be 12 rolls per pan. Once risen to at least double in size, bake at 350 degrees for 15 - 20 minutes, or until golden brown. Brush with melted butter once removed from the oven. While the rolls are baking, make the

icing. Mix together in a saucepan the sugar, sour cream, orange juice, butter and orange zest. Bring the mixture to a boil over medium heat and boil for 3 minutes. Remove from heat. Once rolls are removed from oven, while still hot, pour icing over rolls.

Zucchini Bread

Yields 1 loaf

6 lg	eggs
3½ cups	sugar
1¾ cups	vegetable oil
5 cups	grated zucchini (about 2 zucchinis)
1 Tbsp	vanilla extract
6 cups	flour
2 tsp	salt
2 tsp	baking soda
½ tsp	baking powder
2 Tbsp	ground cinnamon
2 cups	walnuts, chopped
¼ cup	vegetable oil

Preheat the oven to 350 degrees. Grease a large loaf pan heavily with butter. In a large mixing bowl, beat the eggs with an electric mixer until pale yellow in color. Add the sugar and mix well. Add the oil and vanilla extract and mix well. Stir in the zucchini. In a medium mixing bowl, blend the flour, salt, baking soda, baking powder and cinnamon. Add the flour mixture to the egg mixture one cup at a time until it is all blended. Stir in the walnuts and vegetable oil. Bake for 30-40 minutes or until a toothpick stuck in the middle of the loaf comes out with a few crumbs on it.

Black Bean Soup

Serves 4

2 cans	black beans (14 ounces)
2 Tbsp	olive oil
2 Tbsp	lemon juice
1 dash	cayenne pepper
1 tsp	cumin
1 Tbsp	chopped cilantro
3 Tbsp	cooking sherry
¼ cup	sour cream
1 bunch	green onions, chopped
	salt and white pepper, to taste

In a medium sauce pan, place the black beans, olive oil, lemon juice, cayenne pepper, cumin and cilantro. Cook over a low heat for about 30 minutes. Remove from heat and add sherry. Season with salt and white pepper to taste. Serve warm in bowls, garnished with a dollop of sour cream and green onions.

Champagne Brie Soup

Serves 8-10

½ cup	butter (1 stick)
½ cup	flour
4 cups	chicken stock
3 cups	milk
1 lb	Brie, rind removed
2 cups	brut champagne
	salt and white pepper, to taste

Melt the butter in a medium heavy bottomed sauce pan, and then stir in flour. Cook on low heat for about 3 minutes, stirring constantly. Slowly add the stock while stirring and cook for 4 minutes on moderate heat, then bring to a boil. Lower the heat and simmer for 10 minutes. Add the milk and continue to simmer for a few minutes. Cut the Brie into small pieces. Add the Brie to the mixture and stir until completely melted. Lastly, add the champagne and gently stir. Season the soup with salt and white pepper to taste.

Crab and Shrimp Gumbo

Serves 8

4 cups	water
4	beef bouillon cubes

Roux:

2 Tbsp	flour
3 Tbsp	bacon grease
1 cup	onions, diced
½ lb	bacon, cut into small pieces
2 lbs	frozen cut okra
4 cups	stewed tomatoes
1	bay leave
1 tsp	Italian herbs
2 tsp	Krazy salt
1 tsp	Tabasco sauce
1 lb	shrimp, peeled, deveined, cooked, and cut in half
1 lb	fresh blue lump crab meat, picked clean of shells
½ cup	chives, chopped

In a medium sauce pot, heat the water and the bouillon cubes over medium heat.

To make the Roux: In a large heavy skillet, heat the flour and bacon grease over medium high heat. Stir constantly until mixtures turns dark brown. This process will take 10-15 minutes. Never stop stirring and never leave the skillet unattended. The mixture will burn quickly and it will change colors quickly. I prefer to move the skillet on and off the heat as it changes colors to slow the cooking process as to not burn the roux. Continue the process until the mixture changes from white to light brown to reddish brown to dark brown.

Once the roux is the color that you prefer, add okra and sauté in the roux for 1 minute. Add onions and bacon to hot roux and cook for 1-2 minutes until onions are translucent. Add tomatoes and continue stirring. Slowly add warm beef broth to okra mixture. Be careful the mixture will steam when adding the broth. Once the broth is completely incorporated, add bay leaves and Italian herbs and bring to a boil. Reduce heat to low and simmer uncovered for 3-4 hours. Add 1-4 cups water about once an hour. Taste the gumbo and add Krazy salt and Tabasco to taste. Add shrimp and crabmeat about 10 minutes before serving. Serve over white rice and garnish with chives.

Add additional beef bouillon cubes if desired and season with salt and white pepper. Add the mixed vegetables and add water to bring the pot up to ¾ full. Cover and cook over low heat for about 1 hour. Taste and adjust seasonings one more time. If the soup has fat on top, you may want to skim it off at this point. Add potatoes and continue cooking on low for 30 more minutes to 1 hour. Refrigerate any unused portion and serve the next day. I think it is almost better the second day. Serve warm.

NOTE: Starting with cold water is very important as it allows the bones to heat slowly and release the wonderful marrow and flavor inside. If you cannot find soup bones, ask the butcher, or use short ribs.

Homemade Beef Vegetable Soup
Serves 10-12

6 qts	cold water
1 pkg	soup bones (2-3)
2 lbs	beef roast, cubed
1 lg	can diced tomatoes (28 ounces)
4	beef bouillon cubes
2	bay leaves
1 Tbsp	Italian herbs
1 lb	frozen mixed vegetables (corn, peas, carrots, lima beans)
2 lbs	new potatoes, diced
	salt and white pepper, to taste

In a large, heavy bottomed 8 quart or larger stock pot, place the cold water. Place soup bones in the cold water and heat on high until water comes to a boil. Reduce heat to medium and continue cooking for about 1 hour. If you have the time, an additional hour of just water and bones will add a lot of flavor to your soup. Add the cubed beef to the pot and add additional water to bring the water level back to about ¾ full. Increase heat to high and bring to a boil. Reduce heat to medium and cook for about 1 hour. Remove the soup bones with a slotted spoon and discard (or cool and give to your dogs. My dogs love soup day as much as I do.) Add the canned tomatoes, bouillon cubes, bay leaves, and herbs to the pot. Cover pot and cook on low heat for about 1-2 hours. Continue to add water, as the soup cooks down, to bring the level back to ¾ full. Taste for seasonings at this point.

Iced Watercress Vichyssoise
Serves 6

¼ cup	butter (½ stick)
3	leeks, whites only, trimmed, and sliced
1 lg	yellow onion, diced
4 med	russet potatoes, peeled and diced
4 cups	chicken broth
1 bunch	watercress, chopped
2 cups	milk
1 cup	heavy cream
1 bunch	chives, chopped
	salt and white pepper, to taste

In a large heavy bottomed skillet with a lid, melt the butter. Add leeks, onions, and potatoes. Stir until coated with butter. Reduce heat to low and place top on skillet. Cook vegetables by "sweating" them, until tender and soft. This will take about 10-15 minutes. Add chicken broth and simmer for an additional 10-15 minutes. Remove from heat. Pour mixture into blender or food processor, and puree the mixture until smooth. Add watercress and blend until smooth. Pour mixture through a very tight sieve, China cap or chinois into a clean bowl. Use a spoon to help press the solids through the sieve and release the full flavors. Once the mixture is strained, discard of anything left in the sieve. Stir the milk and heavy cream into the potato soup. Seasoned salt and white pepper to taste. Chill for at least 3 hours in the freezer or back of the refrigerator. This soup should be served extra cold and garnish with chives.

Kentucky Cheese Bisque

Serves 8

½ cup	butter (1 stick)
½ cup	onion, finely chopped
½ cup	carrots, finely chopped
½ cup	celery, finely chopped
¼ cup	flour
2 cups	chicken broth
1½ cups	dark beer
1 cup	Cheddar cheese
½ cup	Gouda cheese
3 cups	Velveeta cheese
2 cups	heavy cream
½ tsp	dry mustard
½ tsp	Worcestershire sauce

Melt butter in a medium heavy bottomed stockpot over medium heat. Then add onions, carrots and celery. Sauté the vegetables until they are soft and translucent. Stir in the flour and cook for about 5 minutes. Add chicken broth and beer and increase the heat to high. Bring the mixture to a boil. Once boiling, slowly add cheddar, Gouda and Velveeta cheeses and continue stirring until all the cheese has melted and the soup has returned to a boil. Add the heavy cream, mustard and Worcestershire. Reduce heat to low and cook until thickened. This will take about 10 minutes.

Serve warm in shot glasses or bowls with citrus crème fraîche, candied bacon and a long chive.

CITRUS CRÈME FRAÎCHE

Serves 8

½ cup	sour cream
½ cup	heavy cream, whipped to stiff peaks
2 Tbsp	grated orange peel

Add all three ingredients together and mix well. Serve chilled.

CANDIED BACON

Serves 8

1 lb	bacon, thin sliced
¼ tsp	black pepper
1 cup	light brown sugar
¼ cup	light corn syrup

Mix the black pepper and light brown sugar in a small bowl. Preheat the oven to 300 degrees. Cover a baking sheet pan with parchment paper (or foil) and place a baking rack in the pan. Arrange the bacon in a single layer on top of the baking rack. Sprinkle the sugar and black pepper mixture over the bacon. Then, drizzle with light corn syrup. Place the tray in the center of the oven and bake for 10 minutes. Turn bacon over and return to oven for another 10 minutes. Bacon is done when golden brown and crispy. If the bacon is not done, do not increase the heat. Instead, continue cooking and check every 5 minutes; because of the sugar, the bacon will burn easily. Once the bacon is cooked, transfer to a clean pan with parchment paper to drain and dry completely. Store in an airtight container in the refrigerator for up to two weeks.

Lemon, Artichoke and Chive Soup

Serves 8

3 cloves	garlic, minced
1 sm	shallot, minced
2 Tbsp	olive oil
3 cups	canned artichoke hearts, drained and chopped
4 cups	heavy cream
1 cup	chicken stock
½ cup	dry white wine
1 tsp	lemon zest
2 Tbsp	lemon juice
¼ cup	parsley, chopped fine
¼ bunch	chives, for garnish
	salt and white pepper, to taste

In a medium heavy bottom stock pot, sauté garlic and shallots in olive oil until translucent. Add all remaining ingredients except chives and bring to a boil. Reduce heat and simmer for 30-45 minutes until soup has reduced by about ⅓. Remove from heat and allow to cool slightly. Place mixture in a blender and blend until smooth. Pour mixture through a fine sieve, China cap or chinois. Use a spoon to help press the solids through the sieve. Season the soup with salt and white pepper to taste. Serve chilled or warm. Garnish with chives.

Tomato Basil Soup

Serves 4

2 cups	store bought marinara sauce
	(I like Original Ragu, but others are also fine)
½ cup	sour cream
1 cup	heavy cream
1 Tbsp	dried basil
1 tsp	garlic powder
4	leaves fresh basil

Whisk together all ingredients in a mixing bowl except for the fresh basil. Refrigerate for 2 or more hours, if serving chilled. To serve warm, heat in a medium sauce pot over medium heat for 15 minutes or until the soup is hot all the way through. Garnish with basil chiffonades.

NOTE: Chiffonade: Is the French term that means "made of rags." Generally, lettuces and fresh herbs are used to chiffonade. Remove the basil or other large leaf herb from the stem. Stack 3 or 4 leaves on top of each other and roll into a tight log. With a very sharp knife, cut the basil roll into very thin slices. When unrolled you will have "rags" of herbs. Use immediately.

Blonde Bloody Mary's

Serves 6

1 cup	Yellow Tomato Coulis (see recipe below)
1 cup	high quality vodka (my personal favorite is Grey Goose)
1 Tbsp	white Worcestershire sauce
1 Tbsp	horseradish, grated
1 tsp	green Tabasco hot sauce
1 tsp	salt
1 tsp	lemon juice
1 tsp	lime juice

Garnish:

6	stalks celery
6	pickled okra
6	Queen olives stuffed with a pimento

Mix all ingredients well. Add more Tabasco and horseradish if more spiciness is desired. Serve over ice garnished with a celery stalk, pickled okra, and an olive.

YELLOW TOMATO COULIS

Yields 1 cup

1 Tbsp	extra virgin olive oil
1 lb	yellow cherry tomatoes (or pear, or vine)— cut into pieces
½ tsp	sea salt
2 tsp	white balsamic vinegar (or white wine vinegar)

In a medium skillet, heat the olive oil over medium heat. Add tomatoes and sauté until the tomatoes are soft, about 2-3 minutes. Remove from heat and add the vinegar and salt. Allow mixture to cool for 5-10 minutes. Put mixture in a blender and puree until smooth. Pour through a sieve (or fine strainer) into a bowl and press on the solids with a spoon to release all the liquids into the bowl. May store in the refrigerator covered, for two days.

Brandy Milk Punch

Serves 8

1 cup	high quality brandy or cognac (I like Courvoisier VSOP)
3 Tbsp	sugar
2 cups	half and half
2 tsp	vanilla extract
1	fresh nutmeg, grated; for garnish

In a pitcher, add the brandy and sugar. Stir until all of the sugar is dissolved. Then, add the half and half and vanilla extract. Stir well. Pour into a highball glass filled with crushed ice. Garnish with fresh grated nutmeg. If you like it a little sweeter, add 1-2 additional tablespoons of sugar.

NOTE: A substitute for half and half is equal parts heavy cream and whole milk.

Dark Rum, Tonic with Lime

Serves 1

2 oz	dark or golden rum (my favorites are Myers and Mount Gay)
4 oz	tonic water
1 wedge	lime

Fill a double old fashioned glass with ice. Pour rum over the ice and fill with tonic water until it reaches the top of the glass. Squeeze a lime wedge into the mixture and add the lime to the drink. Stir well and enjoy.

Grapefruit Prosecco Sparkler

Serves 8

1 bottle	chilled Prosecco (may use dry sparkling wine or champagne)
2 cups	chilled pink grapefruit juice, fresh or bottled
½ cup	chilled club soda
8 sprigs	mint (for garnish)

Mix the Prosecco, grapefruit juice and club soda together in a pitcher. Serve in champagne flutes and garnish with mint. For a sweeter drink replace club soda with Sprite (or 7-up).

Hot Wassail

Serves 10

8 cups	apple juice
3 cups	dry Sherry (approximately one bottle)
1 cup	sugar
½ tsp	grated nutmeg
½ tsp	ground ginger
½ tsp	ground allspice
2 sticks	cinnamon

Garnish: Roasted Apples

10 sm	Granny Smith apples or Lady apples, cored
½ cup	brown sugar
¼ cup	water

Preheat the oven to 350 degrees. Combine all of the ingredients in a large stock pot. Heat over medium heat until very warm. Do not allow mixture to boil. Once warm, reduce heat to simmer until ready to serve. Remove the cinnamon sticks and serve warm in small punch cups garnished with apples. While Wassail is warming, place apples on a baking sheet and fill the centers with sugar. Pour water onto bottom of baking sheet. Bake for 20-30 minutes until tender. Remove from oven and cool slightly. Serve as garnish with Wassail.

NOTE: Wassail means "be in good health" in Norse and was originally a toast. The drink was created to complete the toast. Thus, "Wassail, Wassail" my friends. Here's to you.

Mango Margaritas

Serves 6

6 oz	frozen limeade
1 cup	water
¾ cup	high quality tequila (Patron is a great choice)
¼ cup	mango puree (purchased at store or made fresh with recipe below)

Place the limeade, water, tequila and mango puree in a blender. Fill the blender with ice and blend until the mixture is smooth. Pour into a margarita glass rimmed with sugar.

NOTE: To add to the festivity, rim the glasses in colored sugar. The margaritas are a beautiful bright yellow orange color. Compliment this with green or hot pink sugar that can be purchased at local grocery stores in the cake decorating/baking section.

Tequila is not my friend and for those of you who may suffer the same consequence, you may substitute rum for tequila. Very yummy and now you have a Mango Daiquiri.

MANGO PUREE

Serves 1 cup

1 cup	mango, fresh, jarred or frozen, cubed
½ cup	water
½ cup	sugar

Place the cubed mango, water and sugar in a medium saucepan. Heat over medium heat and bring the mixture to a boil. Continue to boil for about 3 minutes. Remove the mixture from the heat and allow to cool for about 5 minutes. Place the mixture in a blender and puree until smooth. Once pureed, return to the saucepan and bring to a boil. Continue boiling until the mixture is reduced by half.

Mint Juleps

Serves 10

1 cup	water
1 cup	sugar
2 bunches	mint, rinsed with cold water
4 cups	high quality Kentucky bourbon
	(Maker's Mark is what I use)
1/3 cup	powdered sugar—for garnish

In a medium, heavy bottomed saucepan, combine the water and sugar. Heat over medium heat until the sugar is dissolved. Increase heat, bring mixture to a boil and cook for 1-2 minutes. Remove the pan from the heat, and add 1 bunch of mint, leaves and stems. Allow the mixture to rest for 30 minutes-1 hour. Remove the mint leaves and cool completely. Place ½ cup of the syrup and the bourbon into a glass pitcher. Stir well and refrigerate. With the remaining bunch of mint, remove the stems and separate into small sprigs. Fill a small glass bowl with water and ice cubes. Place the mint sprigs in the bowl to keep them fresh and perky. Place one sprig of mint in the bottom of a silver mint julep cup or double Old Fashioned glass. Fill the cups with crushed or shaved ice all the way to the top or even over the top, especially if using shaved ice. Pour the cooled bourbon mixture over the ice and mint, and garnish with another sprig of mint on top. Sprinkle with the powdered sugar and serve with a straw. A great refreshing drink for a hot day, even if you are not having a Kentucky Derby Party.

Orange Pomegranate Granita

Serves 6

5 cups	orange juice
½ cup	pomegranate juice

Mix the orange juice and pomegranate juice in a medium-large mixing bowl or pitcher. Pour the mixture into a 2 quart glass baking dish. The liquid should not be more than about 1 inch high on the side of the dish. Place the mixture in the freezer uncovered. After 45 minutes, use a fork and scrape the mixture down the length of the dish several times. Place the mixture back into the freezer. Repeat the scraping process once an hour for the next 3-4 hours or until the mixture is completely frozen and flakey. Hold in the freezer for up to two days until ready to serve. Serve in a small shot glass or small glass. Garnish with a fresh orange wedge and Candied Orange Zest.

Strawberry Lemonade

Serves 8

2 pints	strawberries, green tops removed
1 can	frozen lemonade concentrate (12 ounce can, thawed)
3 cups	cold water
1 cup	strawberries, sliced
1	lemon, sliced

Place the 2 pints of strawberries in a blender and blend on high until pureed. Add the lemonade concentrate and water to the blender. Mix until well blended. Pour the mixture into a pitcher and refrigerate until ready to serve. When ready to serve, garnish glasses or pitcher with sliced strawberries and lemons. Serve very cold.

NOTE: If the lemonade is too tart for your taste, add additional water.

Vodka Gimlets, Ice Cold
Serves 8

2 cups	*high quality vodka (my preference is Grey Goose)*
½ cup	*fresh squeezed lime juice*
½ cup	*Simple Sugar Syrup (see recipe below)*
8	*Candied Lime Slice (see recipe below)*

Place vodka, lime juice and simple syrup in a cocktail shaker. Fill the shaker with ice. Shake vigorously for about 30 seconds and pour over additional crushed ice in a silver goblet (or double Old Fashioned glass). Be sure to serve very cold and garnish with a candied lime slice.

SIMPLE SYRUP
Serves 8

½ cup	*sugar*
½ cup	*water*

Place sugar and water in a small saucepan and heat over medium heat until sugar is completely dissolved. Reduce to low and heat for additional 5 minutes. Remove from heat and allow to cool completely. Store in the refrigerator, covered, for up to one week.

CANDIED CITRUS SLICES
Yields 6-8 slices

1 lg	*orange, lemon, lime or grapefruit*
1 cup	*sugar*
1 cup	*water*
½ cup	*granulated sugar*

Wash and dry the citrus fruits. Slice the fruit into thin rounds. Place sugar and water in a medium saucepan and heat over medium heat until sugar is dissolved. Increase heat and bring mixture to a boil. Once boiling, reduce the heat to low and add the citrus slices. The slices may overlap each other in the water. Continue heating the citrus slices over low heat for 30-40 minutes until the peel becomes translucent. Do not allow the mixture to boil once the citrus have been added. Remove the pot from the heat and allow to cool for about 10 minutes. Remove the slices from the liquid with a slotted spoon and place on a baking sheet to cool.

Watermelon Lemonade

Serves 8

1 med	*seedless watermelon, peeled and cubed*
1 can	*frozen lemonade concentrate*
	(12 ounce can), thawed
3 cups	*cold water*
¾ cup	*cantaloupe, diced small*
¾ cup	*pineapple, diced small*
1 cup	*strawberries, diced small*
1	*lime—sliced; for garnish*
1	*lemon—sliced; for garnish*
1	*orange—sliced; for garnish*

Place the watermelon cubes and any juice in a mixing bowl. Use a spoon and smash the watermelon until mushy. (I put on gloves and use my hands. It is much easier and much more fun.) Place the watermelon water and pulp into a pitcher and add the lemonade concentrate and water. Stir well. Taste for sweetness and tartness. If you desire more sweetness, add ½ cup of sugar and stir until completely dissolved. If the mixture it too tart, add ½ cup water. Add the diced cantaloupe, pineapple, and strawberries. Serve very cold. If possible, refrigerate the lemonade with fruit for 8-12 hours. Serve in tall glasses with slices of orange, lemon and lime.

Baby Spinach, Baby Arugula and Radicchio, Shaved Parmesan, Seared Duck Breast, Orange Segments, Orange Vinaigrette and Duck Cracklings

Serves 8

2	boneless duck breasts with skin
½ pound	baby spinach, cleaned
½ pound	baby arugula, cleaned
1 head	radicchio, sliced
½ cup	shaved Parmesan cheese
3	oranges, segmented
1 cup	Orange Vinaigrette (see recipe p. 233)

Preheat the oven to 350 degrees. Score the skin of the duck breast into small squares without cutting into the breasts. The skin will look like a checker board. Place the duck breasts in a skillet, over medium heat, skin side down. Cook the breast for 5–10 minutes until the skin is slightly crispy. Then, place the duck breasts, skin side up, on a baking pan. Pour all of the remaining fat from the pan over the breasts. Roast in the oven for 15–20 minutes for rare and 30 minutes for medium. Remove duck from oven and allow to cool for 10 minutes. Remove the skin from the breasts with a knife and set aside. Slice duck breasts into thin slices. To make the duck cracklings, dice the skin into small pieces and place in a skillet, over medium heat. Cook the duck skin until very crispy. Be careful not to burn the skin. When done, drain on a paper towel. To assemble salad, place spinach, arugula and radicchio on the plate. Top with orange segments, sliced duck breasts and Parmesan cheese. Drizzle with dressing and top with duck cracklings.

Caramelized Duck Breast Salad

Serves 8

4	boneless duck breast
1 lb	spring greens
1 cup	hazelnuts (filberts), toasted
1	wedge parmesan cheese
8	sprigs thyme
1 cup	dark cherries
1 cup	red wine
1 cup	water
1 cup	sugar
2 cups	thyme balsamic vinaigrette
	salt and black pepper, to taste

Duck:
Trim excess fat from the duck breasts. Heat a large heavy skillet over high heat until very hot. Pat duck breasts dry with a paper towel and season with salt and pepper. Score the duck breasts. Put the breasts skin side down in a skillet and reduce the heat to moderate. Cook the duck breasts for about 20 minutes, or until skin is crisp and golden brown. Turn breasts over and cook about 2 more minutes for medium doneness. Remove from the heat and slice into thin slices.

Poached Cherries:
In a medium heavy saucepan, heat the red wine, water and sugar until boiling over high heat. Add the cherries and boil for 3-5 minutes. Reduce heat and simmer for 20 minutes. Allow to cool in the liquid.

Parmesan:
Take the wedge of Parmesan cheese. Using a vegetable peeler, drag slowly along the side of the wedge to create long, thin pieces. Make at least 8 pieces.

Salad:
Arrange spring greens on 8 plates. Place about ½ of a duck breast, sliced, over the greens. Garnish with poached cherries, toasted hazelnuts, and Parmesan cheese. Drizzle with thyme balsamic vinaigrette and top with a fresh thyme sprig.

Citrus Salad

Serves 6

2 heads	Bibb lettuce (also known as butter leaf or Boston lettuce)
1 cup	orange segments
1 cup	grapefruit segments
½ cup	bacon, cooked and crumbled
1	avocado, peeled, seeded and sliced
1½ cups	Mom's Vinaigrette (see recipe p. 234)

Wash the Bibb lettuce and separate into leaves. Select 6 pretty leaves to use as cups on your plate. Tear the rest of the lettuce into smaller pieces and place into lettuce cups. Arrange the orange segments and grapefruit segments over the lettuce. Sprinkle with the crumbled bacon. Place the avocado slices on top of the salad at the last minute and drizzle with the dressing.

Dijon New Potato and Haricots Verts Salad

Serves 8

2 lbs	baby new potatoes, cut into halves or quarters
½ cup	olive oil
	kosher salt and black pepper
1 lb	green beans
¼ cup	lemon zest
½ cup	Dijon Vinaigrette (see recipe p. 233)
1 cup	Chili Walnuts (see recipe)

Preheat oven to 400 degrees. Toss potatoes in olive oil, salt and black pepper and place on a baking pan. Make sure potatoes are in a single layer. Roast in the oven for 45 minutes until golden brown and fork tender. Fill a stock pot ¾ full of water and bring to a boil. Once boiling, add green beans and cook for 3-5 minutes. Once cooked, drain the green beans from the hot water and cool to room temperature. When potatoes are done, remove from oven and cool completely. Toss with green beans and Dijon vinaigrette. Season with salt and pepper to taste. Right before serving, garnish with chili walnuts and lemon zest.

CHILI WALNUTS

Yields 1 cup

1 cup	walnut halves
¼ lb	butter (1 stick)
¼ cup	Worcestershire sauce
½ tsp	dried Italian seasonings
½ tsp	dried thyme
½ tsp	sea salt
¼ tsp	cayenne pepper

Preheat the oven to 300 degrees. Place butter, Worcestershire, Italian seasonings, thyme, sea salt and cayenne pepper in a small sauce pan. Warm and stir until well blended. Remove from the heat. Add walnuts to the butter mixture and toss until well coated. Place the walnuts on a sheet pan and bake for 10-15 minutes, until toasted. Store in an airtight container in the refrigerator for up to two weeks.

Field Greens, Baby Spinach and Fresh Herbs Salad

Serves 8

1 lb	Spring greens
½ lb	baby spinach
¼ cup	parsley leaves
⅛ cup	cilantro leaves
¼ cup	basil leaves
2	blood oranges, peeled and segmented
8	Black Mission figs (or Turkish figs), cut in half
½ cup	crumbled feta cheese
½ cup	Herb Roasted Pecan pieces (see recipe p. 227)
½ cup	pistachios, toasted
2 cups	Blood Orange Vinaigrette (see recipe p. 233)

Layer all ingredients in a salad bowl. Serve with blood orange vinaigrette.

HERB ROASTED PECANS

Yields 2 cups

2 cups	pecans, halves or pieces
¼ cup	butter (½ stick)
1 tsp	dried Italian herbs
½ tsp	salt

In a medium skillet, melt the butter over low heat. Add the pecans and sauté until they look toasted, about 5 minutes. Keep the heat low so you do not burn the nuts. Remove the pan from the heat and toss with salt and herbs. Spread the pecans on a baking sheet lined with parchment paper and allow to dry. Keep in an air tight container at room temperature until ready to use.

Fresh Fruit Skewers

Serves 8

16	6 inch wooden skewers
1	cantaloupe, cubed or balled
1	honeydew melon, cubed or balled
1	pineapple, cubed or balled
2 pints	strawberries, stemmed and whole
1 cup	Poppy Seed Dressing (see recipe p. 234)

Assemble the skewers by placing one cube of pineapple, cantaloupe, and honeydew on one end. On the other end, place 1 strawberry. Serve on a platter with poppy seed dressing as a dipping sauce.

Gourmand Salad

Serves 8

2 heads	hearts of romaine lettuce, washed and torn into small pieces
1 lb	baby spinach, cleaned
1 pt	grape tomatoes (or cherry, halved)
2 lg	yellow bell pepper, roasted and sliced
2 lg	ripe avocados, sliced
1 cup	quartered artichoke hearts
1 lg	cucumber, peeled and sliced thin
½ cup	pine nuts, toasted
½ cup	crumbled bleu cheese
1½ cups	Champagne Vinaigrette (see recipe p. 233)

In a large serving bowl, layer ½ of the romaine and ½ of the spinach. Top with ½ of all of the ingredients except the dressing. Repeat with a second layer. Refrigerate until ready to use. You may refrigerate for up to two hours. When ready to serve, drizzle the vinaigrette on the salad in concentric circles around the greens. You may substitute feta cheese for bleu cheese if you prefer.

Harvest Salad

Serves 8

6 oz	plain goat cheese
2 Tbsp	fresh assorted herbs (basil, oregano, chive), minced
1 med	pomegranate
1 lb	spring greens
1 med	granny smith apple, sliced thin, soaked in orange juice
½ cup	dried cranberries
2 cups	Sweet Vinaigrette (see recipe p. 233)

Form the goat cheese into a small log and roll in the minced fresh herbs. Slice log into 8 slices. If you do not have access to fresh herbs, you may substitute 1 tablespoon of dried Italian herbs. Cut the pomegranate in half and use your hands to remove the seeds from the white pith. If you have gloves, use them because the pomegranate juice will stain your hands. The seeds will easily come loose. Store the seeds in the refrigerator until ready to use for up to three days. When ready to assemble the salad, place ½ of the greens in a salad serving bowl. Add half of the cranberries, pomegranate seeds and the apple slices to the top of the greens. Repeat and add the goat cheese slices on the top. Dress the salad with sweet vinaigrette by drizzling the dressing in concentric circles around the greens.

Heart Salad

Serves 8

2 heads	hearts of romaine
1 cup	sliced hearts of palm
1 cup	quartered artichoke hearts
3 lg	Roma tomatoes, sliced
½ cup	bleu cheese crumbles
1 cup	Mom's Vinaigrette (see recipe p. 234)

In a serving bowl, place all of the lettuce and layer the hearts of palm, artichoke hearts and Roma tomato slices on top of the lettuce. Sprinkle the bleu cheese over the tomatoes. When ready to serve, drizzle the dressing in concentric circles over the salad.

Individual Caesar Salad

Serves 8

2 heads	romaine lettuce, washed, leaves separated and left whole
1 cup	seasoned croutons
¼ cup	shredded Parmesan cheese
¼ cup	fresh lemon juice
¼ cup	powdered Parmesan cheese
1 Tbsp	coarse grain mustard
1 Tbsp	Dijon mustard
1 clove	garlic, minced
1 tsp	Worcestershire sauce
⅓ tsp	Tabasco
1 cup	extra virgin olive oil

Take the leaves from one head of romaine and tear into small pieces. Place the whole leaves on a serving platter. Fill the whole leaves with the small pieces of lettuce. Top with croutons and shredded Parmesan cheese. To make the dressing, combine the lemon juice, powdered Parmesan cheese, mustards, garlic, Worcestershire and Tabasco in a blender. Remove the blender lid. Blend the ingredients until well mixed and then slowly pour the oil in a steady stream. Taste and add more olive oil if desired. When ready to serve, pour the dressing over the romaine leaves and serve.

Melon Salad with Lavender Syrup

Serves 6

1	cantaloupe, cut into cubes or balls
1	honeydew melon, cut into cubes or balls
1 sm	seedless watermelon, cut into cubes or balls
½ cup	Lavender Syrup (see recipe below)

Place all three melons in a serving bowl. Drizzle with lavender syrup and serve chilled. Garnish with fresh lavender.

LAVENDER SYRUP

½ cup	sugar
½ cup	water
2 Tbsp	dried lavender

Place all in small pot. Bring to a boil for 1 minute. Cool and strain. Serve chilled.

Mexican Mango Salad

Serves 8

1 head	romaine, washed and torn into small pieces
1 head	red leaf lettuce, washed and torn into small pieces
½ cup	diced red onions
½ cup	frozen corn
1 cup	diced red bell peppers
1 cup	mangos, diced
½ cup	crumbled blue cheese
½ cup	toasted walnuts
2 cups	Mango Vinaigrette (see recipe p. 234)

In a medium serving bowl, place ½ of the lettuces and top with ½ of each ingredient except the dressing. Repeat this step. Cover with plastic wrap and refrigerate for up to 6 hours until ready to serve. When ready to serve, drizzle with dressing in concentric circles over salad.

NOTE: If you cannot find fresh mangos, often you can find them in jars in the refrigerated section of the grocery store.

Orange Cilantro Slaw

Serves 8

1 med	red onion, cut into thin slivers
1	bunch cilantro, chopped
2 med	carrots, cut into thin slivers
½ med	red cabbage, cut into thin slivers
½ med	green cabbage, cut into thin slivers
1 tsp	orange zest
½ cup	orange juice
1 Tbsp	white wine vinegar
½ cup	vegetable oil
2	whole oranges, segmented
¼ cup	whole cilantro leaves
	Kosher salt and white pepper, to taste

In a large mixing bowl, mix together the onions, cilantro, carrots, and red and green cabbage. In a separate bowl, blend together the orange zest, orange juice, vinegar and the oil. Pour the dressing over the vegetables and toss well. Season the slaw with kosher salt and white pepper to taste. Refrigerate until ready to serve. This may be made up to 4 hours ahead of time. The salad and the dressing can be made the day before and not mixed until about 2 hours prior to serving. Serve very cold and garnish with orange segments and cilantro leaves.

Pepper Crusted Beef Tenderloin Salad

Serves 8

Pepper Crusted Beef Tenderloin:

1	whole beef tenderloin (4-5 pounds), trimmed of all fat
1 Tbsp	Beau Monde (or celery salt)
¼ cup	cracked black pepper
½ cup	Worcestershire sauce
½ cup	butter (1 stick), melted

Salad:

1 lb	baby arugula
1 lb	baby spinach
2 lg	red tomatoes
2 lg	yellow tomatoes
1 pint	yellow tear drop tomatoes, halved
1 pint	grape tomatoes, halved
½ lb	fresh mozzarella, sliced
1	bunch fresh basil
1 cup	Mom's Vinaigrette (see recipe p. 234)

Beef:

Preheat oven to 450 degrees. Heavily season the beef with Beau Monde. Then, rub with cracked black pepper. Place beef in roasting pan and cook for 20-25 minutes until the internal temperature is 120 degrees. Remove from oven and pour Worcestershire and butter over the hot beef. Let beef cool for 20-30 minutes and then refrigerate up to 24 hours. Just before serving, slice beef into ½ inch thick slices.

Salad:

Mix spinach and baby arugula and arrange on a serving platter or plate. Layer the slices of beef tenderloin, tomatoes, mozzarella and basil over the greens. Alternate the slices so that you have beef, tomato, mozzarella, basil etc. Drizzle with dressing and garnish with grape tomato halves. Season with salt and pepper as desired.

Red Wine Poached Cranberry Salad

Serves 8

1 cup	dried sweetened cranberries (Craisins)
½ cup	sugar
1 cup	red wine
½ lb	spring green
1 cup	toasted pecan halves
1 cup	crumbled feta
2 cups	Cranberry Vinaigrette (see recipe p. 233)

Place the cranberries in a medium sauce pan with the sugar and red wine. Bring the mixture to a boil over medium heat. Reduce the heat to a simmer and cook for 15-20 minutes. Remove from heat and cool. Layer the salad greens with cranberries, pecans, and feta cheese in a salad bowl. Refrigerate until ready to serve. When ready to serve drizzle dressing in concentric circles over the salad greens.

Roasted New Potato Salad with Bacon, Bleu Cheese and Lemon Zest

Serves 8

2 lbs	small new potatoes, cut in half
½ cup	olive oil
2 Tbsp	olive oil
½ cup	country Dijon mustard
1 cup	crumbled bacon
¼ cup	crumbled bleu cheese
¼ cup	diced chives
1 Tbsp	lemon zest, long strips
	Kosher salt and black pepper, to taste

Preheat oven to 400 degrees. Toss potatoes in ½ cup olive oil, salt and pepper. Roast for 45 minutes until golden brown and fork tender. Remove potatoes from the oven and cool to room temperature. Blend together 2 tablespoons olive oil and country Dijon. Toss potatoes in the mixture. Season the salad with salt and pepper to taste. Refrigerate until ready to serve. Garnish the top with bacon, bleu cheese, chives and lemon zest.

Roma Halves with Diced Heirloom Tomato, Avocado and Jicama Salad

Serves 8

4	whole Roma tomatoes, halved lengthwise
4 med	heirloom tomatoes (various colors), diced
1	jicama, peeled and diced
½ cup	olive oil
3 Tbsp	fresh orange juice
3	basil leaves, chopped
2	avocados, diced
8	whole basil leaves

Scoop out the meat and seeds of each tomato half. Turn the tomato cups upside down on a pan and drain for 20-30 minutes. In a mixing bowl, stir together the heirloom tomatoes and jicama. Drizzle with olive oil, orange juice and chopped basil. Season with salt and pepper to taste. Spoon filling into tomato cups and refrigerate for up to an hour, or until ready to serve. Garnish with diced avocado and whole basil leaves.

Spring Green Salad with Raspberries, Blueberries, Bleu Cheese, and Toasted Pecans

Serves 8

½ lb	spring greens
1 pt	raspberries
1 pt	blueberries
1 cup	bleu cheese
1 cup	toasted pecans
1 pt	Raspberry Vinaigrette (see recipe p. 233)

Layer all ingredients in a serving bowl. Drizzle the greens with dressing in concentric circles when ready to serve.

Stone Fresh Fruit Salad

Serves 8

2 lg	peaches, peeled and sliced
1 cup	red cherries, pitted and cut in half
1 cup	yellow cherries, pitted and cut in half
2 lg	nectarines, sliced
2	apricots, sliced
6	sprigs fresh mint, chopped
6	sprigs fresh basil, chopped
¼ cup	sugar

Place all the fruits in a mixing bowl. Add the mint and basil and toss until well mixed. Add the sugar, mix well and refrigerate for one hour before serving.

Sunset Salad

Serves 4

2 cans	small green beans
1 can	sliced water chestnuts
1 can	quartered artichoke hearts
1 sm	jar pimentos
2 cups	Mom's Vinaigrette (see recipe p. 234)

Layer all ingredients in a salad bowl. Pour dressing over the ingredients and marinate overnight, if possible. Serve chilled.

Sweet Corn and Tomato Salad

Yields 3 cups

4 med	Roma tomatoes, finely chopped
1 cup	sweet corn kernels
⅔ cup	red onion, finely chopped
¼ cup	Italian parsley, chopped
¼ cup	extra virgin olive oil
3 Tbsp	fresh lemon juice
	salt and black pepper, to taste

Combine tomatoes, corn, red onions, parsley, olive oil and lemon juice in a medium bowl. Season with salt and black pepper to taste. Refrigerate until ready to use or up to 12 hours.

Watermelon, Peaches, and Blueberries

Serves 8

1 sm	seedless watermelon
1 pt	blueberries
10	peaches (or 1 pound of frozen peach slices), peeled and sliced
¼ cup	sugar

Peel watermelon and cut into cubes or balls. Put melon into a bowl and mix with blueberries and peaches. Sprinkle with sugar and toss well. Serve chilled.

Zesty Caribbean Salad

Serves 8

1	head green leaf lettuce, washed and torn into small pieces
1	head bibb lettuce, washed and torn into small pieces
2 lg	oranges, peeled and segmented
2 lg	kiwis, peeled and sliced
1 lg	starfruit, washed and sliced
1 lg	avocado, peeled and sliced
½ cup	Jerk Spiced Cashews (see recipe below)
½ cup	bacon, cooked crisp and crumbled
1 cup	Coriander Lime Vinaigrette (see recipe p. 233)

In a medium serving bowl, place ½ of the lettuces and top with ½ of each ingredient except the dressing. Repeat this step. Drizzle with dressing in concentric circles over the lettuce and serve.

JERK SPICED CASHEWS

Yields 3 cups

Jerk Seasoning:

2 tsp	onion powder
1 tsp	dried thyme
1 tsp	ground allspice
1 tsp	salt
1 tsp	chili powder
½ tsp	garlic powder
½ tsp	table grind black pepper
¼ tsp	ground cinnamon
¼ tsp	cayenne pepper
¼ tsp	cumin
¼ cup	sugar
3 cups	raw cashews
2 Tbsp	vegetable oil

Preheat the oven to 200 degrees. Mix all of the seasoning in a bowl, except for the cashews vegetable oil. Sprinkle 2 tablespoons of the jerk seasoning over the cashews and toss with oil until well coated. Place the nuts on a baking sheet lined with parchment paper. Bake the nuts in the oven for about 20 minutes, until the nuts are crispy. Remove the sheet from the oven and allow the nuts to cool completely. Store in an airtight container until ready to use.

Salad Dressings

Sweet Vinaigrette (Base Recipe)

Yields 2 cups

½ cup	red wine vinegar
½ cup	sugar
½ tsp	garlic powder
½ tsp	salt
½ tsp	onion powder
½ tsp	black pepper
½ tsp	dry mustard
1 cup	vegetable oil

Place all ingredients in the blender except the oil. Turn the blender on high and blend until smooth. Remove the small cap from the blender lid and slowly pour the oil into the mixture in a steady stream. The dressing will become velvety and creamy. Taste and adjust for seasonings.

Variations: Many of my dressings came from this original recipe that was shared with me by Clare Casademont. It is my favorite dressing after Mom's Vinaigrette.

Blood Orange Vinaigrette: Substitute red wine vinegar with white wine vinegar and add ¼ cup blood orange juice and 2 tablespoons lemon juice

Cranberry Vinaigrette: Reduce red wine vinegar to ¼ cup and add ¼ cup cranberry juice

Orange Vinaigrette: Substitute red wine vinegar with white wine vinegar and add ¼ cup orange juice

Orange Lime Vinaigrette: Substitute red wine vinegar with white wine vinegar and add ¼ cup orange juice and 1 tablespoon fresh lime juice

Raspberry: Substitute red wine vinegar with raspberry vinegar and add ½ cup frozen or fresh raspberries; if you cannot find raspberry vinegar, use red wine vinegar and add another ½ cup raspberries

Sherry Vinaigrette: Reduce red wine vinegar to ¼ cup and add ¼ cup dry sherry and reduce sugar to ¼ cup.

Champagne Vinaigrette (Base Recipe)

Yields 3 cups

½	clove garlic
1	shallot
½ tsp	dry mustard
1 Tbsp	fresh herbs (basil, parsley, thyme, oregano, and tarragon)
½ cup	white wine vinegar
¼ cup	dry champagne
2 cups	vegetable oil
	kosher salt and white pepper, to taste

Place all ingredients in a blender, except the oil. Blend all ingredients well. While the blender is still running, remove the middle portion of the top and slowly drizzle the oil into the blender until the dressing is emulsified and thick. Stop the blender and taste for salt and pepper. Feel free to add another ¼ cup of oil if your desired consistency is not reached. The more oil you add the thicker the dressing will be.

Variations: This is another base vinaigrette recipe that I use for many dressings.

Balsamic Vinaigrette: Substitute dry mustard with 1½ teaspoons Dijon, take herbs out all together and substitute white vinegar with balsamic vinegar and champagne with red wine.

Dijon Vinaigrette: Substitute dry mustard with 1½ tablespoons Dijon and substitute champagne with 2 tablespoons lemon juice.

Coriander Lime Vinaigrette: Add ½ teaspoon dried ground coriander and substitute champagne with fresh lime juice.

Thyme Balsamic Vinaigrette: Instead of all herbs use only thyme and substitute white wine vinegar with balsamic vinegar.

Mango Vinaigrette

Yields 2 cups

½ cup	red wine vinegar
½ cup	honey
½ cup	mango juice, (the juice from jarred mangoes)
2	slices jarred mango
1 Tbsp	dried Italian seasoning
1 tsp	Dijon mustard
½ tsp	paprika
1 cup	vegetable oil

Place all ingredients in the blender except the oil. Turn the blender on high and blend until smooth. Remove the filter cap in the blender lid and slowly pour the oil into the mixture in a steady stream. The dressing will become velvety and creamy. Taste and adjust for seasonings.

Mom's Vinaigrette

Yields 2 cups

1 med	onion, finely chopped
1 tsp	sugar
1 tsp	salt
1 tsp	celery salt
¼ cup	red wine vinegar
¾ cup	olive oil

In a large mixing bowl, place the onions, sugar, salt, celery salt and the red wine vinegar. Stir well. Refrigerate for 1 hour. Using a whisk, whisk in the olive oil until well incorporated. This will keep in the refrigerator for up to three weeks.

Poppy Seed Dressing

Yields 2 cups

⅓ cup	white wine vinegar
1 Tbsp	white sugar
4 Tbsp	honey
½ tsp	salt
1 cup	vegetable oil
3 Tbsp	poppy seeds

Place the vinegar and sugar in the blender, and blend until the sugar is completely dissolved. Add honey and salt and blend for 30 seconds. Remove the filter cap in the blender lid. Slowly add oil while the blender is running. Dressing will thicken quickly. Pour dressing into a bowl and add poppy seeds. Stir gently.

Caribbean Chicken
with Lime Coconut Butter

Serves 6

1 Tbsp	butter
1 Tbsp	flour
1 Tbsp	minced onions
1 tsp	minced garlic
¼ tsp	minced jalapeno
¼ cup	chicken broth
¼ cup	unsweetened coconut milk
½ cup	heavy cream
1 tsp	lime juice
½ cup	sliced hearts of palm
½ cup	diced fresh tomatoes
2 lbs	chicken breasts, skinless and boneless
1 cup	flour
1 cup	butter (2 sticks)
1 Tbsp	chopped cilantro
	salt and white pepper, to taste

Preheat the oven to 200 degrees. In a heavy bottomed medium saucepan, heat butter over medium heat. Add flour and stir for about 2 more minutes. Do not allow the roux to brown. Add the onions and sauté until translucent. Add the garlic and jalapenos and sauté for 2 minutes. Add the chicken broth, coconut milk and heavy cream. Bring mixture to a boil and reduce heat to simmer. Allow to simmer for about 5 minutes. Add the lime juice, hearts of palm and tomatoes. Adjust seasonings with salt and white pepper.

Rinse the chicken breasts and slice each breast in half, then in half again. Place a piece of plastic wrap (or parchment paper) on a cutting board. Place a piece of the chicken on the plastic and place another piece of plastic (or parchment) on top of the chicken. Using a rubber mallet (or small heavy skillet), pound the breast until it is very thin but not falling apart. Remove the pieces of the chicken, dredge through the flour, and place on a platter. Heat butter in a heavy bottomed skillet over medium heat until it is melted and hot. Work in small batches and place the pieces of pounded chicken into the hot butter and cook for about 2-3 minutes on each side. Cook until the chicken is no longer pink inside and is golden brown on the outside. Place the cooked chicken in a baking dish and cover with sauce. Place the dish in the oven for up to 30 minutes and hold until ready to serve. When ready to serve, garnish with cilantro.

Chicken Crepes Provence

Serves 12

24	Crepes (store bought or make dinner crepes) (see recipe p. 207)
3 lbs	boneless, skinless chicken breast
1 cup	olive oil
⅛ tsp	salt
⅛ tsp	white pepper
1½ lbs	mushrooms, sliced
2 Tbsp	butter
¼ cup	chopped chives

Make the sherry cream sauce, listed at right. Preheat the oven to 375 degrees. Place chicken breasts in a baking pan and drizzle with olive oil and season with salt and white pepper. Bake the chicken breasts for 20-30 minutes until breasts are no longer pink inside. Remove from oven and cool completely. Dice chicken into small cubes. Slice the mushrooms and sauté them in butter in a medium, heavy bottomed saucepan. Toss the diced chicken, sautéed mushrooms and a little bit of the sherry cream sauce together in a mixing bowl. Spray a glass baking dish with food release or Pam. Lay crepes out on a work space and place ¼ cup of filling into the middle of each crepe. Roll the crepe around the filling. Drizzle additional sauce over the crepes and bake in oven for 20 to 25 minutes until bubbly. Top with chopped chives and serve warm.

SHERRY CREAM SAUCE
Yields 3 cups

2 Tbsp	butter
2 Tbsp	flour
2 cups	heavy cream
2 Tbsp	dry white wine
1 Tbsp	cooking sherry
½ cup	butter, cold
	salt and white pepper, to taste

In a medium, heavy bottomed sauce pan, combine the flour and butter and cook over medium heat for about 5 minutes, stirring constantly. Add in the heavy cream, white wine and sherry. Stir to combine. Heat the mixture until almost boiling, while continually whisking until a smooth, thick consistency is reached. Cut the butter into small pieces and whisk into the mixture. Simmer until the mixture is thickened and coats the back of a wooden spoon. Season sauce with salt and white pepper.

Chili Lime Flank Steak with Tropical Fruit Salsa
Serves 12

4 lbs	flank steak, trimmed of any visible fat
1 cup	orange juice
½ cup	freshly squeezed lime juice
6 Tbsp	ketchup
½ cup	vegetable oil
¼ cup	honey
6 Tbsp	soy sauce
6 Tbsp	chili powder
3 Tbsp	horseradish
2 Tbsp	minced garlic
1 tsp	cayenne pepper
1 Tbsp	salt
1 lg	lemon, thinly sliced
1 lg	orange, thinly sliced
1 lg	lime, thinly sliced
1	bunch cilantro, chopped

Place the flank steak in a large, glass baking dish. In a mixing bowl, create the marinade by mixing together the orange juice, lime juice, ketchup, vegetable oil, honey, soy sauce, chili powder, garlic, horseradish, cayenne, and salt. Stir well. Layer the orange, lemon and lime slices over the flank steak. Pour the marinade over the meat. Cover with plastic wrap and refrigerate over night. This really needs to marinate for at least 12 hours for the flavors to soak into the meat. You may also marinate the meat in Ziplock baggies, if you prefer. When ready to cook the meat, preheat a grill to a very high temperature. If you are using a charcoal grill, make sure that the coals have turned gray before placing the meat on the grill. Remove the meat from the marinade and discard the marinade. Place the flank steak on the grill, 1-2 pieces at a time, and grill over very hot heat. Grill for 2-3 minutes on each side. The meat should be medium rare, approximately 120 degrees internal temperature. Remove the meat from the grill and allow to rest at room temperature for 15 minutes. Slice the flank steak very thinly, against the grain of the meat and on a diagonal, as you cut through the meat. This will assist the meat in being very tender. Serve the flank steak on platter at room temperature with tropical fruit salsa, listed below. Garnish with cilantro.

NOTE: If you do not like things spicy, cut back on the chili powder and cayenne.

TROPICAL AND SPICY FRUIT SALSA
Yields 6 cups

2 cups	pineapple, diced
2 lg	kiwis, diced
2 cups	mango, cubed
¼ cup	red bell pepper, diced
¼ cup	yellow bell pepper, diced
¼ cup	green bell pepper, diced
¼ cup	white wine vinegar
½ tsp	red pepper flakes
⅛ cup	cilantro, minced
2 Tbsp	sugar

To make the salsa, mix all the ingredients together in a mixing bowl, and cover with plastic wrap. Refrigerate for at least 2-3 hours, or over night.

Classic Chicken Salad
Serves 8

2½ lbs	chicken breasts, boneless, skinless, remove any fat and gristle
2 Tbsp	olive oil
1 cup	lemon parsley mayonnaise
	salt and black pepper, to taste

Lemon Parsley Mayonnaise:

2½ cups	Hellman's mayonnaise
¾ tsp	Krazy salt (or season salt)
½ tsp	table grind black pepper
4 Tbsp	lemon juice
2 Tbsp	finely minced fresh parsley

Bring a pot of water to a rolling boil. Add the chicken breasts to the water and continue to boil for about 15 minutes. Be sure to cook the chicken breasts completely. Cut a breast open and if any of the meat is even slightly pink, return to the water and continue to boil until cooked all the way through. Remove the chicken from the water and cool to room temperature. Cut into ½ inch cubes. Toss the chicken cubes in the olive oil and refrigerate until completely cool. Do not add the mayonnaise to warm chicken. In a medium mixing bowl, combine mayonnaise, Krazy salt, pepper, lemon juice and parsley, and mix well. Refrigerate until ready to use. Once the chicken is completely cooled, toss in lemon parsley mayonnaise and adjust salt and pepper to taste. It is best to make the chicken salad the day before and refrigerate over night. Keep in refrigerator for up to two days.

Dijon and Herb Crusted Double Rack Lamb Chops with Cabernet Demi Glace
Serves 12

24	purple or white pearl onions
½ cup	butter (1 stick)
6	rack of lamb (14-16 ounces each), Frenched
6 Tbsp	Dijon mustard
3 Tbsp	dried Italian herbs

Bring a pot of water to a boil. Place onions with skin in the water for 2-3 minutes. Remove from the water and cool slightly.

Use a small knife to peel. Melt the butter in a skillet and sauté the onions for 5-7 minutes, or until fork tender.

Preheat oven to 400 degrees. Season the lamb with salt and black pepper. Rub the lamb with Dijon mustard. Heavily, pat the lamb with the Italian herbs on top of the Dijon mustard. Bake the lamb in the oven for 20-25 minutes, until it reaches an internal temperature of 130 degrees.

CABERNET DEMI-GLACE
Yields 2 cups

1 cup	demi-glace (can be purchased at store)
½ cup	cabernet sauvignon wine
1 Tbsp	red wine vinegar

Place all of the ingredients in a heavy bottomed, sauce pan and stir well. Heat over medium heat and bring to a boil. Reduce heat to simmer, and cook for 20 minutes. Serve warm.

Eggs Benedict Crepes
Serves 10

20	Crepes (store bought or make dinner crepes) (see recipe p. 207)

Filling:

20	eggs
2 cups	heavy cream
1 cup	Canadian bacon (or ham), finely diced
½ cup	snipped chives

Preheat oven to 350 degrees. In a mixing bowl, blend the eggs and cream until slightly frothy. Heat a large, heavy bottomed skillet over medium heat. When hot, add eggs and stir until cooked but not dry. Remove from heat and add diced Canadian bacon or ham. Spray two glass baking dishes with food spray or Pam. Place crepes out on a work surface. Place about ¼ cup of the egg mixture in the middle of each crepe. Roll the crepes around the filling, and place the crepes seam side down in the pan. Each pan should hold 10 crepes. Cover the pans with wax paper and foil. Place in the oven and heat for 20-30 minutes. Remove crepes from oven and make the hollandaise sauce.

Spoon hollandaise over the crepes, and garnish with chives and serve immediately.

HOLLANDAISE SAUCE
Yields 1 cup

½ cup	butter (1 stick)
2	egg yolks
1 pinch	salt
⅛ tsp	dry mustard
1 Tbsp	lemon juice
1 Tbsp	white wine

Heat the butter in a medium, heavy bottomed sauce pan until bubbly. Combine all other ingredients in a blender. With the blender turned on, pour the hot butter slowly into the yolk mixture in a slow, steady stream. The mixture will become very thick.

Ela's Southern Style Fried Chicken
Serves 4

1	whole chicken (2-3 pounds), cut into 8 pieces
2 Tbsp	Lawry's seasoned salt
1 tsp	black pepper
2 lg	eggs, beaten
1 cup	whole milk
2 cups	flour
4 cups	vegetable oil

Season the chicken with seasoned salt and pepper. Mix eggs and milk together, and pour over the chicken. Refrigerate the chicken in a milk mixture for 1-2 hours. Place flour in a large bowl and sprinkle with a little extra season salt. Heat the oil, in a large cast iron skillet, to 350 degrees or until the oil begins to ripple. Start with breasts and toss in flour mixture one piece at a time until well covered. Shake excess flour from chicken and carefully place chicken in hot oil with skin side down. When one side is golden brown, turn over and cook on other side until golden brown. Move breasts to the side while still in the oil and add the thighs, then drumsticks and wings last. Cook all pieces on both sides until golden brown. Reduce the heat to low and continue cooking. The breasts will take about 20-25 minutes. Thighs and legs will take 15 minutes to cook. Wings take about

10 minutes. Use a small knife and make a small cut or prick on the breasts. Remove chicken from oil and drain chicken on paper towels. Serve warm.

Grilled Baby Back Ribs with Spicy Bourbon Barbeque Sauce
Serves 6

Spice Rub:

3 Tbsp	cumin
2 Tbsp	kosher salt
1 Tbsp	dry mustard
1 Tbsp	chili powder
2 tsp	cayenne
1 tsp	cinnamon
1 tsp	white pepper
½ tsp	cardamom
½ tsp	allspice
3	racks baby back pork ribs (2 pounds each)

Mix together in a small bowl all the spices for the rub. Rub the spice mixture onto the ribs, approximately 2 tablespoons per rack. Be sure to put the mixture on both sides of the ribs. Arrange racks single layer on a baking sheet, cover in plastic wrap and refrigerate overnight. When ready to cook ribs, prepare a charcoal or gas grill. If using charcoal, prepare a very hot fire and make sure the coals have turned gray before putting the ribs on the fire. Place the racks on the grill and cook for about 20 minutes and turn ribs over and cook another 20 minutes on the other side. The ribs are done when the meat is fork tender. Remove the ribs from the grill and place on a clean baking sheet. Brush with barbeque sauce. Return the ribs to the grill for approximately 10 minutes until the sauce caramelizes on the ribs. Slice ribs and serve with additional bourbon barbecue sauce. See recipe next page.

SPICY BOURBON BARBEQUE SAUCE
Yields 12 cups

¼ cup	vegetable oil
2 cups	yellow onions, chopped
1 cup	green onions, chopped
¼ cup	minced garlic
2 med	jalapenos, seeded and chopped
1 Tbsp	cumin
1 Tbsp	chili powder
1 tsp	cayenne pepper
1½ cups	brown sugar
½ cup	honey
2 cups	ketchup
½ cup	tomato paste
½ cup	yellow mustard
1 Tbsp	Tabasco sauce
1 cup	water
½ cup	Worcestershire sauce
½ cup	white wine vinegar
1 cup	bourbon
	salt and black pepper, to taste

In a large, heavy bottomed sauce pot, heat the vegetable oil and sauté the yellow onions until translucent. Add green onions, garlic and jalapeno peppers and sauté until all vegetables are soft, about 5 minutes. Stir in the cumin, chili powder, cayenne pepper, brown sugar and honey, and cook for 2-3 minutes until sugar is almost dissolved. Add the ketchup, tomato paste, yellow mustard, Tabasco and water. Bring to a boil. Reduce the heat and simmer for 30 minutes. Add Worcestershire and vinegar and simmer for an additional 30-45 minutes until reduced by ⅓. Add bourbon and continue to simmer for additional 30 minutes. Season the sauce with salt and black pepper to taste. This sauce is spicy. If you prefer less spice, use only one jalapeno or remove it all together. Also, reduce the cayenne pepper and white pepper. This can be made a day ahead and refrigerated until ready to use.

Grilled Chicken Enchiladas with Tomatillo Sauce
Serves 8

2 lbs	chicken breasts, skinless and boneless
1 cup	chopped onions
1 cup	chopped cilantro
½ cup	vegetable oil
16	flour tortillas
3 cups	shredded Monterey jack cheese

Make Tomatillo Sauce (see recipe p. 241). Then, preheat an indoor grill pan until hot. Preheat oven to 350 degrees. Spray 2 glass baking dishes with food release or Pam. Season the chicken with salt and white pepper. Place chicken breasts on hot grill pan and cook for about 2-3 minutes per side until no longer pink on the inside and cooked throughout. Cooking time will depend on thickness of the breast. Remove from heat and cool for 5-10 minutes. When cooled, cut into approximately 1 by 1 inch cubes and set aside. In a medium, heavy bottomed skillet, place the onion and cilantro and heat covered over low. Heat until onions are translucent, about 10 minutes. In a heavy bottomed, medium skillet, heat the oil over medium heat for about 2 minutes. Once the oil is hot, using tongs place the tortillas, in the hot oil, one at a time, for about 15-20 seconds and then turn over and repeat. This process is used to soften the tortillas. Do not leave in the oil too long or they will become very hard, crispy and unable to roll. Remove the tortilla from the oil and drip off excess oil. Place drained tortillas on a plate. Repeat until all tortillas are done. Add more oil as needed. There should be at least ½ an inch of oil in the pan at all times. Stack the tortillas on top of each other on the plate. When ready to assemble, lay out the tortillas on a work space. Spoon about 1 tablespoon of the tomatillo sauce in the middle of each tortilla. Top with 1 teaspoon of the onion cilantro mixture. Add 5-6 cubes of chicken across the middle of the tortillas and top with 2 tablespoons of cheese. Roll tightly and place seam side down in a prepared baking dish. The enchiladas will be snug in the dish. Approximately 8-10 will fit into one dish. Continue until all tortillas are rolled. The enchiladas and sauce may be made ahead and refrigerated at this point for up to one day or frozen for up to 1 month. When ready to serve, preheat the oven to 350 degrees. Pour the sauce over the enchiladas and top with extra shredded cheese. Bake uncovered for 20-30 minutes, until bubbly and hot.

TOMATILLO SAUCE
Yields 1 quart

2 Tbsp	vegetable oil
1 cup	diced red onion
1 Tbsp	minced garlic
½ lb	tomatillos, husk removed and washed
1 sm	can diced green chiles
1	bunch cilantro, chopped
½ cup	heavy cream
	salt and white pepper

In a medium, heavy bottomed sauce pot, heat the vegetable oil. Sauté onions until translucent and then add garlic and cook for additional 2 minutes. Add tomatillos, green chiles and cilantro and sauté for about 4 minutes. Reduce heat to low and simmer for 15 minutes. Remove from heat and cool for about 10 minutes. Place mixture in the food processor and blend until well combined. Return to pot and add cream. Season with salt and white pepper to taste.

Hazelnut Coffee Crusted Rib Eye Roast
Serves 14

1	boneless rib-eye roast of beef (approximately 8-10 pounds)
1½ Tbsp	salt
1 Tbsp	coarsely ground black pepper
½ cup	fine ground hazelnut coffee

Preheat the oven to 325 degrees. Generously season the roast with salt and black pepper. Then, press the coffee grinds onto the outside of the roast. Place the roast in a roasting pan, fat side up, and roast the meat for 2½ -3 hours (or until meat reaches an internal temperature of 130 degrees). Remove from oven and rest for 10-15 minutes before slicing. The coffee adds additional flavor and the bitterness balances nicely with the fat from the roast. Serve with Cabernet Black Truffle Morel Reduction (see recipe).

CABERNET BLACK TRUFFLE AND MOREL REDUCTION
Yields 4 cups

3 Tbsp	butter
⅓ cup	finely chopped shallots
1 oz	fresh black truffle, finely diced (or 1 Tbsp black truffle oil)
12	fresh morel mushrooms or dried and rehydrated
2 cups	dry red wine
2 cups	demi-glace (can be purchased at store)
1 Tbsp	balsamic vinegar
	salt and black pepper, to taste

In a heavy bottomed, medium skillet, sauté the shallots in the butter, for about 5 minutes. Add the truffles and morels and cook for 5 additional minutes. Stir in red wine and bring to a boil. Reduce heat to medium and cook until the mixture is reduced by half, about 15 minutes. Add the demi-glace and cook for an additional 15 minutes. Remove pan from the heat and stir in balsamic vinegar. Season the reduction with salt and black pepper to taste.

Kentucky Pulled Pork
Serves 10

1	pork butt (5-6 pounds; bone-out)

Rub:

1 Tbsp	paprika
1 Tbsp	brown sugar
1 tsp	beau monde (or celery salt)
½ tsp	garlic powder
½ tsp	dry mustard
½ tsp	onion powder
½ tsp	table grind black powder
¾ tsp	salt
¼ tsp	cinnamon

Mix all of the rub ingredients together in a bowl. Using gloves, rub the mixture onto the pork butt. Cover in plastic wrap and refrigerate for 3-4 hours.

Smoking:

Soak half a bag (or about 8 cups) of hickory chunks in water. Place the chips in a smoker box where they are not over direct heat. Place the pork butt on the grill, not on direct heat. Close the grill and smoke for 6 hours plus. Add charcoal or wood every hour. If pork browns too much, wrap in foil and keep cooking. Remove the pork from the grill and wrap in foil. Allow to cool for 1 hour. Using gloves pull the pork into shreds. Serve drizzled with Raspberry Chipotle Sauce (see recipe below).

RASPBERRY CHIPOTLE SAUCE
Yields 1¼ cup

¼ cup	*marinated chipotle peppers, diced*
1 cup	*raspberry preserves*

Blend raspberry preserves and peppers in a food processor. Refrigerate until ready to serve.

Leg of Lamb, Herb de Provence Crusted
Serves 10

1	*whole boneless leg of lamb (about 4-5 pounds), excess fat removed*
½ cup	*olive oil*
½ cup	*Dijon mustard*
½ cup	*Herb de Provence*

Preheat oven to 450 degrees. Season the boneless leg of lamb with salt and black pepper. Mix the olive oil and mustard together in a small bowl and spread mixture on lamb. Sprinkle generously with dried herbs. Bake for 20 minutes, then reduce heat to 375 degrees and continue cooking for 30-40 minutes (until lamb has reached an internal temperature of 140 degrees). Remove from oven and rest at room temperature for 10 minutes before slicing. Serve with Bing Cherry and Kumquat Compote (see recipe).

BING CHERRY AND KUMQUAT COMPOTE
Yields 4 cups

1 cup	*water*
1 cup	*sugar*
¼ lb	*kumquats (about 10), cut in half lengthwise*
3 cups	*fresh bing cherries (or dark red cherries), pitted*

In a small, heavy saucepan, bring water and sugar to a boil. Boil for 2-3 minutes. Add kumquats and simmer for 5 minutes. Remove kumquats with a slotted spoon. Add cherries to the sugar mixture and simmer for 10 minutes. Remove from heat and cool mixture completely. Add kumquats back to the mixture right before serving. Serve warm or cold.

Mom's Meatloaf
Serves 10

2 lbs	*high quality ground beef*
1 tsp	*salt*
½ tsp	*ground black pepper*
1 cup	*oatmeal*
1½ cups	*chopped onion*
3	*eggs, beaten*
1 can	*tomato sauce (14 ounces)*
3 slices	*bacon*

Preheat oven to 350 degrees. Sauté onions in a small sauce pan until translucent. In a mixing bowl, mix together beef, salt, pepper, oatmeal, onion and eggs. Form mixture into a long and wide log about the same size as a loaf pan. Pour tomato sauce on top and lay strips of bacon on top. Bake for 1-1½ hours. Make sure the meat is not pink on the inside. Serve warm.

Oven Roasted Beef Tender
Serves 12

1	whole beef tenderloin (5-6 pounds), trimmed of all fat
2 Tbsp	beau monde (or celery salt)
2 Tbsp	black pepper
½ cup	butter (1 stick), melted
1 cup	Worcestershire sauce

Preheat oven to 450 degrees. Heavily season the beef tenderloin with beau monde and black pepper. Bake the beef tender in the oven for 20-30 minutes, until beef reaches an internal temperature of 120 degrees for medium rare (130 degrees for medium or 140 degrees for medium well). When the tenderloin is done, remove from oven and cover with Worcestershire sauce and melted butter. Allow meat to rest for 15-20 minutes. Slice and serve with Secret Sauce or Horseradish crema (see recipe).

SECRET SAUCE
Yields 2 cups

¼ cup	bleu cheese, crumbled
1 Tbsp	Worcestershire sauce
1 Tbsp	A-1 steak sauce
1 tsp	red wine vinegar
1 tsp	lemon juice
1 cup	butter (2 sticks), cold and cut into slices

In a medium saucepan, over medium heat, combine bleu cheese crumbles, Worcestershire sauce, A-1 sauce, red wine vinegar and lemon juice. Cook for about 5 minutes until cheese has melted and is bubbly. Remove from heat and whisk in the butter one piece at a time until all butter is combined.

Oven Roasted Turkey
Serves 16-18

1 lg	turkey (18-20 pounds), completely thawed
1	orange
1	onion
½ lb	butter (2 sticks), melted
4 Tbsp	beau monde (or celery salt)
1 Tbsp	flour
1	roasting bag

Preheat the oven to 325 degrees. Make sure your turkey is completely thawed or it will not cook properly. Allow the turkey to thaw in the refrigerator for 3-4 days or thaw in the sink under cold running water for a couple of hours. Rinse both cavities (top and bottom) well and remove the neck, liver, and gizzards. Place the turkey in a roasting pan.

Clean the sink well with soap and hot water. Always clean utensils, sink, and work space very well after working with raw turkey. Season the turkey with beau monde (or celery salt). Cut the orange and onion in half. Place half of an orange in the front cavity and the other half with both onion halves in the back large cavity. Toss 1 tablespoon of flour in the roasting bag then add turkey. Pour melted butter over the turkey and close the bag. Place the whole bag in the roasting pan. Bake for about 3-3½ hours (approximately 10 minute per pound of turkey). Make to test your turkey with an ainstant read thermometer in many places. Turkey should have an internal temperature of at least 170 degrees. Remove the turkey from the oven and allow to rest in the bag for about 15-20 minutes. Remove the turkey from the bag and place on a platter. Decorate and serve. Serve with Brown Gravy and Cranberry Orange Relish (see recipe below).

BROWN GRAVY

Yields 1 quart

½ cup	flour
½ cup	butter (1 stick)
3 cups	chicken stock
	salt and black pepper, to taste

Sauté flour and butter in a large, heavy skillet over medium heat. Stir constantly until the mixture becomes medium to dark brown. This will take about 10-12 minutes. Be careful not to burn. Slowly add the chicken stock to the mixture. Be careful, the mixture will bubble and steam. Season the gravy with salt and black pepper to taste.

CRANBERRY ORANGE RELISH

Yields 1 quart

1 lb	fresh cranberries
1	whole orange, cut into small pieces
2 cups	water
1½ cups	sugar
¼ cup	orange marmalade

Wash the cranberries and place in medium sauce pan with oranges and water. Bring the mixture to a boil over high heat, and then reduce heat to simmer. Simmer uncovered for 20 minutes. Cool the mixture for 10-15 minutes. Place the mixture in a food processor and pulse until just pureed. Return the mixture to the pan and add the sugar and orange marmalade. Bring the mixture to a boil and continue boiling for 5-6 minutes. Cool completely and refrigerate.

Secret Beef and Cheese Enchiladas with Red Sauce

Serves 8

NOTE: Sauce and enchiladas can be made ahead of time and frozen until ready to use. I make an extra large batch of sauce and then get it out of freezer when I want to make enchiladas.

Red Sauce:

⅓ cup	oil
⅓ cup	flour
2 Tbsp	chili powder
1 Tbsp	garlic powder
1 tsp	powdered beef broth base
1 tsp	cumin powder
½ tsp	coriander
1 tsp	salt
2 cups	tomato sauce
5 cups	boiling water

Enchiladas:

½ cup	vegetable oil
16	corn tortillas
½ lb	ground beef, cooked and drained
3 cups	cheddar cheese, shredded
1 cup	Monterey jack cheese, shredded
1 cup	minced onion

In a medium, heavy bottomed sauce pan, heat the oil for 1 minute over medium heat and slowly stir in the flour to make a paste. Add the chili powder, garlic powder, powdered beef base, cumin powder, coriander and salt. Slowly add the tomato sauce to the mixture. Add the boiling water and stir until well incorporated. Bring the sauce to a boil and reduce heat to simmer. Cook uncovered for 1-1½ hours until sauce has reduced by at least ⅓. While the sauce is cooking, in a heavy bottomed, medium skillet, heat the oil over medium heat for 2 minutes. Once the oil is hot, using tongs, place the tortillas one at a time in the hot oil for about 15-20 seconds and then turn over and repeat. This process is used to just soften the tortillas. Do not leave in the oil too long or they will become very hard and crispy and will not roll. Remove the tortilla from the oil and place on a plate. Repeat until all tortillas are done. Add more oil as needed. There should be at least ½ inch of oil in the pan at all times. Stack the tortillas on top of each other on the plate. In a separate mixing bowl, combine together the beef, cheese, and onion. When ready to assemble, lay out the tortillas on a work space. Spoon about 1 tablespoon of sauce on each tortilla. Top the sauce with ¼ cup of cheese mixture. Roll tightly and place seam side down in a glass or metal baking dish. The enchiladas will be snug in the dish. Approximately 10-12 will fit in one pan. Continue until all tortillas are rolled. The enchiladas and sauce may be made ahead and refrigerated at this point for up to one day. When ready to serve, preheat the oven to 350 degrees. Pour the sauce over the enchiladas, and top with extra grated cheddar cheese. Bake for 20-30 minutes, until bubbly and hot.

Whole Chicken Fried Quail

Serves 2

2 cups	vegetable oil
4	whole quail
1 cup	flour
1 Tbsp	Lawry's seasoned salt
1 tsp	black pepper
1 cup	milk
	salt and black pepper

Preheat the oven to 325 degrees. In a heavy bottom, preferably cast iron skillet, heat the vegetable oil until almost smoking. Reduce heat and wait for 5 minutes. Rinse the quail well and pat dry with a paper towel. Season the quail with salt and pepper. In a glass baking dish, place the flour and the Lawry's salt and black pepper. Put milk into another dish. Dip the quail into the milk and then the flour mixture. Shake to remove excess flour and add to the oil in the skillet. Start with the breast side down. Cook for about 5 minutes on each side. Remove from the skillet and place on paper towels to drain. Place the quail into a clean baking dish and cook in the oven for 10-15 minutes. Serve warm.

Whole Semi-boneless Grilled Quail

Serves 8

1 cup	vegetable oil
½ cup	red wine vinegar
2 Tbsp	sugar
2 tsp	lemon juice
1 tsp	salt
1 tsp	dehydrated onion flakes
1 tsp	dehydrated garlic
½ tsp	red pepper flakes
8 whole	semi-boneless quail

Place all ingredients for marinade in a bowl and mix together. Place the quail in the marinade for 30 minutes-1 hour. Preheat grill on high heat. Place quail on grill, breast side down. Cook for about 3-4 minutes, then turn and grill about 2-3 minutes on the other side. The quail should be golden brown after grilling.

Chilled Seafood: Stone Crab Claws, Marinated Blue Crab Salad, Cold Boiled Shrimp with Tartar Sauce, Spicy Red Sauce, Louie Sauce and Cajun Remoulade

Serves 8

1 lb	stone crab claws, boiled, cracked, shell removed
1 lb	shrimp (16-20 count), boiled, peeled, deveined, tails on

Chill the Stone crab claws and the shrimp for at least 2 hours before serving. Serve with tartar sauce, spicy red sauce, Louie sauce and Cajun remoulade.

MARINATED BLUE CRAB SALAD
Yields 8

1	clove garlic
1	whole shallot
½ tsp	dry mustard
1 Tbsp	fresh tarragon
½ cup	white wine vinegar
¼ cup	dry champagne
2 cups	vegetable oil
1 lb	jumbo lump Blue crab meat
1 Tbsp	Hellman's mayonnaise
	kosher salt and white pepper

Place garlic, shallot, dry mustard, tarragon, vinegar and champagne in a blender and blend on high. While the blender is still running, remove the middle portion of the top and slowly drizzle the oil into the blender until the dressing is emulsified and thick. Stop the blender and taste for salt and pepper. Add another ¼ cup of oil if you want your dressing to be thicker.

Place the blue crab meat in a bowl. Carefully, pick through the crabmeat to remove any shells or debris. I prefer to place the cleaned crabmeat in another bowl. Pour one cup of the champagne tarragon vinaigrette over the crabmeat and toss lightly. Fold in the mayonnaise and season with salt and pepper to taste.

TARTAR SAUCE
Yields 1¼ cups

1 cup	Hellman's mayonnaise
2 Tbsp	pickle relish
¼ cup	onion, minced
1 Tbsp	horseradish

Combine all ingredients; let stand at least 30 minutes before serving.

SPICY RED SAUCE
Yields 2 cups

2 cups	ketchup
1 Tbsp	Worcestershire sauce
4 Tbsp	horseradish
1 tsp	Tabasco sauce

Mix all ingredients together. Refrigerate until ready to serve.

LOUIE SAUCE
Yields 1½ cups

4 oz	cream cheese, softened
½ cup	Thousand Island dressing (store bought)
¼ cup	Hellman's mayonnaise
2 Tbsp	minced pimentos
2 Tbsp	grated onion
2 Tbsp	chopped green onions
2 tsp	Tabasco sauce
1½ tsp	Lawry's seasoned salt
1½ tsp	horseradish

Place softened cream cheese, Thousand Island and mayonnaise in a mixing bowl. Beat with an electric mixer until smooth. Stir in remaining ingredients. Chill for 3-4 hours or overnight.

Braised Baby Vegetables

Serves 8

16	white or purple pearl onions, trimmed and peeled
2 Tbsp	butter
16	baby carrots, peeled and with a ½ inch stem intact
16	brussel sprouts, trimmed
½ cup	vegetable stock
16	baby new potatoes, boiled, peeled, and shaped

Bring a medium pot of water to boil. When boiling, drop pearl onions in and boil for 2-3 minutes until the skin appears loosened. Drain and use a sharp paring knife to remove the other skin. Melt the butter in a medium heavy bottomed skillet over medium heat. Add all vegetables into the pan. Stir until all are covered in butter. Cook for about 5 minutes, then add the stock and bring liquid to a boil. Reduce heat to low, cover and cook the vegetables for another 5-10 minutes until tender. Remove the veggies from the liquid with a slotted spoon. Let the remaining liquid reduce by half. Pour over the veggies before serving.

Buttered Petit Pois

Serves 4

1 lb	petit pois (tiny peas frozen)
¼ cup	butter, melted
½ tsp	Krazy salt

Bring water to a boil in a medium sauce pot. Add peas and bring back to a boil. Stir the peas to separate them. Cook the peas for 5 minutes, or until heated through. Pour into a strainer and drain the water. Return the peas back to the pot and pour the melted butter over them. Toss with Krazy salt and serve.

Caramelized Texas 1015 Onions and Mushrooms

Serves 8

2 med	Texas 1015 onions (or other sweet onion), peeled and sliced
½ cup	butter (1 stick)
2 Tbsp	sugar
1 lb	mushrooms, sliced

Heat the butter in a medium, heavy bottomed skillet over medium heat. Add the onions and cook until translucent. Add sugar and increase heat to high. Cook for 3-4 minutes, until the sugar becomes syrupy and the onions have a nice caramel color. Add mushrooms and saute until mushrooms are soft.

Charred Beans

Serves 8

2 Tbsp	vegetable oil
½	onion, chopped
¼	jalapeno, seeded, deveined and diced
½	clove garlic, minced
1 lg	roasted red bell pepper, diced
2½ cups	chicken stock
2 lbs	canned black beans (with the liquid)
2 tsp	fresh oregano
1½ tsp	ground cumin
½ tsp	ground coriander
1	bay leave
1½ tsp	fresh cilantro
1 Tbsp	dry sherry
	salt and white pepper

In a heavy skillet, sauté the onions in the vegetable oil over medium heat until the onions are translucent. Continue cooking the onions until they are browned and caramel in color. Add the jalapeno, garlic and red peppers, and continue to sauté for 5 minutes. Add chicken stock, black beans, oregano, cumin, coriander and bay leaves. Bring the mixture to a boil then reduce to a simmer. Cook over low heat for 1 hour while stirring periodically. Season the beans with salt and white pepper. Just before serving garnish the beans with cilantro leaves and stir in the sherry.

Cheddar Cheese Grits Soufflé
Serves 12

3 cups	water
½ cup	butter (1 stick)
3 cups	milk
3 cups	quick cooking grits (not instant)
1½ tsp	salt
1½ cups	grated cheddar cheese
2 Tbsp	Worcestershire sauce
1 tsp	Tabasco sauce
3	egg yolks
3	egg whites
¾ cup	grated cheddar

Preheat the oven to 325 degrees. Grease a 9 x 13 glass baking dish with butter. In a medium, sauce pan bring the water, butter and milk to a boil. Once boiling, slowly stir in the grits. Add the salt and reduce the heat to medium-low and cover. Cook until thickened, stirring occasionally, about 5-7 minutes. Remove the pan from the heat. While it's still hot, add the cheddar cheese, Worcestershire sauce and Tabasco. Pour the grits mixture into the prepared baking dish. In a separate bowl, beat the egg yolks until light in color and stir them into the grits. In another bowl, beat egg whites to a soft peak. Immediately, fold the egg whites into the grits. Place the glass dish on a baking sheet with sides. Pour water onto the baking sheet pan until it comes half way up the sides of the grits dish. Cook for 1 hour or until set and lightly browned on top. Top with additional grated cheese before serving.

Consommé Rice Pilaf
Serves 8

3¾ cups	Campbell's beef consommé (about 3 cans)
½ cup	butter (1 stick)
2 cups	white rice

Place the consommé in a medium sauce pan and warm over medium heat to almost boiling. Melt the butter in another 3 quart sauce pan over medium heat. Once the butter is melted, add the rice and sauté for 3-4 minutes, stirring constantly. Do not allow the rice to burn. Add the hot consommé to the rice. Bring the mixture to a boil. Reduce the heat to low, cover, and cook on low heat for approximately 20 minutes. Once the rice is cooked, fluff with a fork. Serve warm.

Creamy Mashed Red Potatoes
Serves 8

3 lbs	small red new potatoes
1 cup	butter (2 sticks), melted
½ cup	heavy cream
1½ tsp	salt
	black pepper

Boil the new potatoes in water in a medium pot until fork tender. Remove from the water and place in a mixing bowl while still hot. Add butter, cream, salt and pepper. Using a hand mixer beat the potatoes until smooth. If you want more cream, butter, or salt, this is the time to add the additional amounts. Serve warm. You may cool the potatoes after beating and reheat later, but you must add the butter and cream immediately after cooking.

Tomato Pie

Serves 6

1	9 inch pre-baked deep dish pie shell
4 lg	red beefsteak tomatoes, sliced
10	fresh basil leaves, chopped
1 cup	Hellman's mayonnaise
1 cup	grated cheddar cheese
1 cup	grated mozzarella cheese
	salt and black pepper

Preheat oven to 350 degrees. Bake the pie shell in the oven for 10 minutes. Lay the tomato slices on a paper towel to drain while pie shell is cooking. Season tomato slices with salt and pepper. Place tomato slices and the basil in the pre-baked pie shell and top with mayonnaise. Sprinkle cheddar cheese and mozzarella cheese on top of the mayonnaise. Bake in oven for about 30 minutes until the pie is lightly browned on the top. Cut into 6 or 8 pieces and serve.

Whipped Sweet Potatoes Served in an Orange Cup

Serves 8

6 lg	sweet potatoes, cooked, peeled, and mashed
4	eggs, beaten
½ cup	light brown sugar
1 cup	butter (2 sticks), melted
2 tsp	salt
2 tsp	cinnamon
1 cup	fresh orange juice
4 lg	oranges
1 cup	pecan pieces
¼ cup	sugar

Preheat the oven to 375 degrees. In a large mixing bowl, place the mashed sweet potatoes. Stir in the eggs, brown sugar and melted butter. Add the salt, cinnamon and orange juice. Beat potatoes with an electric beater until light and fluffy. Place mixture into a glass baking pan. Bake in oven for 20-30 minutes until hot and bubbly. While baking, prepare the orange cups. Cut the oranges in half. Use a small knife and cut around the skin in the inside of the orange between the skin and pulp, Use a spoon and remove the segments, pulp and pith from the orange. You will be left with an orange cup. Remove sweet potatoes from oven and spoon the mixture into the prepared orange halves. Top with pecan pieces and sprinkle with sugar. Place on a baking sheet and return to the oven for 10-15 minutes until pecans are slightly browned.

Wild Rice Salad

Serves 6

2 cups	Uncle Bens long grain and wild rice mixture
1	green bell pepper, diced
3	green onions, finely chopped
½ cup	chopped fresh mint
3	Roma tomatoes, seeded and diced
⅔ cup	chopped and toasted pecans
3 Tbsp	lemon juice
¼ cup	olive oil
½ tsp	black pepper
¼ tsp	salt

Cook rice according to package instructions. Cool the rice on a baking sheet until completely cooled. Transfer the rice to a mixing bowl. Add the green bell peppers, green onions, mint and Roma tomatoes. Stir in the pecans. In a separate small bowl, mix together lemon juice, olive oil, pepper and salt. Drizzle liquid over rice and stir well. Refrigerate until ready to use for up to 6 hours.

Almond Macaroons Dusted with Powdered Sugar

Yields 24 cookies

1 cup	whole blanched almonds
⅔ cup	sugar
1 lg	egg white
½ tsp	almond extract
½ cup	confectioner's sugar, for dusting
1 pinch	salt

Preheat oven to 350 degrees and lightly butter a baking sheet. In a food processor, pulse almonds with sugar until finely ground. Add the egg white, almond extract, and a pinch of salt. Pulse until combined. Remove mixture from food processor and form into 1" balls. Place them on the prepared sheet pan about 2 inches apart. Flatten the balls with a spoon and lightly dust with confectioner's sugar. Bake the macaroons for about 10 minutes or until light golden brown. Cool completely and store in airtight container until ready to serve.

Bananas Foster

Serves 8

1 cup	brown sugar
1 cup	butter (2 sticks)
8 med	bananas, firm
½ cup	white rum (or dark)
8	scoops vanilla ice cream

Place butter and sugar in a large, heavy bottomed skillet over medium heat. While butter and sugar are melting, peel and slice the bananas into butter mixture. Stir until sugar is completely melted and the mixture is vigorously bubbling. Carefully, add the rum. The mixture will create a lot of steam. If cooking on a gas stove, pull the skillet back slightly from flame and the mixture should catch on fire. Stir until the flame extinguishes. Serve over vanilla ice cream. (If cooking on an electric stove, use a long handled lighter to ignite the mixture.)

Bittersweet Chocolate and Dried Cherry Bread Pudding with Amaretto Crème Anglaise

Serves 10

1½ lbs	stale French bread, cubed (2 large baguettes)
1 cup	bittersweet chocolate chips
½ cup	dried cherries
8	whole eggs
8 cups	whole milk
4 cups	sugar
½ cup	butter (1 stick), melted
1½ Tbsp	vanilla extract

Preheat oven to 350 degrees. Butter a 9 x 13 baking pan. Cut bread into cubes. Place the bread cubes in a large mixing bowl. Add the chocolate chips and dried cherries. Toss with your hands. In a separate mixing bowl, beat together the eggs, milk, sugar, butter, and vanilla. Fold liquid mixture into bread, chocolate and cherries. Pour mixture into prepared pan and bake for about 25 minutes. Bread pudding should be lightly browned on top. Check to see if done by gently shaking pan to see if it is still runny. When done, remove from oven and let cool for 5-10 minutes. Serve with Amaretto Crème Anglaise (see recipe below).

AMARETTO CRÈME ANGLAISE

Yields 3 cups

2 cups	whole milk
6 lg	eggs yolks
5 Tbsp	sugar
2 Tbsp	amaretto
1 pinch	sea salt

Place the milk in a heavy sauce pan and heat over medium heat until scalded. (Scalded is a cooking technique where you heat milk or cream to just before boiling.) Remove from heat and set aside. In a mixing bowl, whisk together the egg yolks and the sugar until the mixture is well combined and gradually add hot milk into yolk mixture in a slow steady stream. Whisk constantly until all the milk is incorporated. Return the entire mixture to the sauce pot and cook over medium heat, stirring constantly, with a wooden spoon, until the mixture thickens. This will take about 3 minutes. If you have a candy thermometer, cook until it reads 170-175 degrees. Remove from heat and pour through a fine sieve into a metal bowl that is sitting in another bowl of ice water. Stir until cool. Add amaretto and salt. Cover the sauce and chill for at least 2-3 hours. The sauce can be made up to 3 days in advance.

Blonde Brownies
Serves 8

½ cup	butter (1 stick), melted
1 cup	brown sugar, packed
1	egg
1 cup	flour
1 tsp	baking powder
½ cup	pecans
1 tsp	vanilla extract

Preheat the oven to 350 degrees. Grease an 8 by 8 inch baking pan with butter. In a heavy bottomed sauce pan, melt butter and brown sugar over low heat. Do not allow to boil. Remove from heat and stir in the egg, flour, baking powder, pecans, and vanilla extract. Bake for 20-30 minutes, or until golden brown and set. Cool completely.

Bourbon Pecan Pie
Serves 16

Crust:

2	premade deep dish 9 inch pie crusts

Filling:

6 lg	eggs
2 cups	brown sugar, packed
1⅓ cups	light corn syrup
½ cup	butter (1 stick), melted
¼ cup	bourbon
1 tsp	lemon zest, finely grated
4 cups	pecan halves, toasted, coarsely chopped

Preheat oven to 350 degrees. In a large mixing bowl, whisk together eggs, brown sugar, corn syrup, butter and bourbon. Stir in lemon zest and pecans. Divide the filling into the two pie crusts. Bake pie until the filling is puffed and set in the center, about 45-55 minutes.

Bread Pudding with Maker's Mark Bourbon Sauce

Serves 8-10

2	loaves baguettes, (about 10 cups), torn into small pieces about 1" square
½ cup	butter (1 stick), melted
8 cups	whole milk
8 lg	whole eggs, beaten
4 cups	sugar
1½ Tbsp	vanilla extract
2	egg whites
1 tsp	ground cinnamon

Preheat the oven to 350 degrees. Grease a 15 x 10 glass baking dish with butter. Place the torn bread in large mixing bowl, and add the butter, milk, beaten eggs, sugar, and vanilla. Using a spoon or your hands, mix well and mash the bread until mushy. In another bowl, beat the egg whites until they form stiff peaks. Gently fold the egg whites into bread mixture. Pour filling into the prepared pan and bake for 45 minutes-1 hour, or until golden brown on top. Sprinkle with cinnamon and serve with Maker's Mark Bourbon Sauce (see recipe below).

MAKER'S MARK BOURBON SAUCE

Yields 2 cups

4	egg yolks
½ cup	powdered sugar
½ cup	Maker's Mark bourbon
1½ cups	heavy cream

In a large mixing bowl, beat the egg yolks until light yellow in color. Add the powdered sugar and whiskey. Stir until well incorporated. In a heavy bottomed sauce pan, warm the heavy cream until scalded. Slowly stir into the egg mixture. Serve warm over the bread pudding.

Brownie Cake Bites Dipped in Chocolate

Serves 8

1 cup	butter (2 sticks), cut into ½ inch pieces
8 oz	semisweet chocolate, chopped
2 oz	unsweetened chocolate, chopped
3	eggs
1 cup	sugar
2 tsp	vanilla extract
¾ cup	flour
1 tsp	baking powder
1 cup	semisweet chocolate chips, for dipping
1 pkg 6	inch wooden skewers

Preheat oven to 350 degrees. Line a 9 x 13 baking pan with parchment paper. Combine both chocolates and butter in the top of double boiler over simmering water and stir until chocolate is completely melted. Remove from the double boiler and cool slightly. In a large mixing bowl, beat together the eggs, sugar and vanilla with an electric mixer. In another bowl, combine the flour, baking powder and salt. Combine flour into the egg mixture a little at a time until well incorporated. Stir in the chocolate mixture and transfer batter to the prepared pan. Cook in the oven for 20-25 minutes, until set. Remove from oven and cool completely. Cut into 1 x 1 inch squares. Melt the semisweet chocolate chips in a glass bowl in the microwave for 30 second intervals until melted. Place each brownie on a 6 inch wooden skewer and dip into the melted chocolate. Place onto a baking sheet and cool.

Caramel, White and Dark Chocolate Dipped Apples Rolled in Popcorn

Serves 8

4 lg	granny smith apples, washed and dried
4 lg	red delicious apples, washed and dried
24	caramel candies, Brach's
2 cups	plain popcorn, popped
2 cups	semisweet chocolate chips
2 cups	white baking chocolate, chopped
8	wooden skewers

Place the skewers into the stems of the apples. Line a baking sheet pan with lightly buttered wax paper (or parchment paper). Heat the caramel candies in a heavy bottomed sauce pan over low heat and cook until melted. Remove from heat and dip each apple into the warm caramel sauce and swirl them to coat completely. Allow the excess caramel to drip off the apples. Hold the apple for about 15-20 seconds before placing on the buttered baking sheet. Spread the popped popcorn on a baking sheet. Roll the caramel dipped apples in the popcorn. Press the apples lightly into the popcorn to help it stick. Allow the apples to stand for about 30 minutes to allow the caramel to set. Place the semisweet chocolate chips in a glass bowl and heat in the microwave on high for 30 seconds at a time until the chocolate is completely melted. Separately melt the white chocolate in the same manner. Be very careful to not get any water in the chocolate or the consistency of the chocolate will change. Use a spoon and drizzle about one teaspoon of each chocolate on the caramel dipped apples. Place the apple back on the tray with the greased wax paper to dry. Allow to dry for about 30 minutes before serving. Cut apples into 8 pieces and arrange on a tray.

Cherry Peach Napoleon
Serves 6

2 cups	caramelized peaches
2 cups	cherry créme brulée
12	Bing cherries (or dark red), pitted and halved
12	Rainier cherries, pitted and halved
2 cups	peach sorbet
6	almond lace cookies
6 Tbsp	lavender peach reduction

Place about 2-3 tablespoons of caramelized peaches in a brandy snifter (or other wide mouth glass). Spoon 2-3 tablespoons of cherry custard on top of peaches and add 4 halves of each type of cherry. Refrigerate until ready to serve. When ready to serve, drizzle cherries with 1 tablespoon lavender peach reduction and top with one scoop of peach sorbet. Garnish with almond lace cookie and serve immediately.

NOTE: If you are unable to find fresh cherries, you can use frozen Dark Red Cherries.

CARAMELIZED PEACHES
Yields 2 cups

6 Tbsp	butter
3 Tbsp	brown sugar
6	fresh Texas or Georgia peaches, peeled, pitted and diced (or 2 cups frozen peaches)

Melt the butter in a heavy bottomed skillet over medium heat. Add the brown sugar and the peaches and stir until the sugar is dissolved and the mixture begins to bubble. Reduce the heat to low and stir occasionally for about 5 minutes. The peaches will become tender and the caramel sauce will have a syrup consistency. Remove from heat and allow to cool to room temperature.

CHERRY CRÈME BRULÉE
Serves 8

½ cup	frozen dark cherries, thawed
1 cup	heavy cream
1 cup	milk
3	egg yolks
½ cup	sugar
1 tsp	cherry liquor

Place the cherries in the blender and blend until smooth. In a heavy bottomed medium sauce pan, add the pureed cherries, heavy cream and milk and heat over medium heat until the cream is scalded (steam is coming off the cream but not boiling.) In a separate large mixing bowl, beat the egg yolks and sugar with an electric mixer until pale yellow in color. Very slowly stir the hot milk mixture into the egg mixture. Make sure you stir constantly so that the eggs do not curdle. Return the mixture to the sauce pan and cook over medium heat, stirring constantly, until the mixture coats the back of a wooden spoon (about 10 minutes). Stir in the cherry liquor. Remove from the heat and allow to cool to room temperature. Place in refrigerator for at least 4 hours before serving.

LAVENDER PEACH REDUCTION
Yields 2 cups

1½ cups	diced frozen peach slices, thawed
1 cup	water
1 cup	sugar
1	bunch fresh lavender leaves,
	(or 2 Tbsp dried lavender flowers)

Place peaches in a blender, and blend on high until smooth. In a medium, heavy bottomed sauce pan, place water and sugar. Bring to a boil over medium heat and stir until the sugar is completely dissolved. Add lavender leaves and the liquid peaches. Reduce the heat to simmer and allow to simmer for 10 minutes or until mixture thickens and becomes syrupy. Remove from heat and cool to room temperature. Pour sauce through a sieve and discard the leaves or flowers. Store in refrigerator until ready to use.

ALMOND LACE COOKIE
Yields 24 cookies

⅛ cup	light corn syrup
⅛ cup	light brown sugar
2 Tbsp	butter
¼ cup	flour
¼ cup	almonds, blanched and sliced
¼ tsp	vanilla extract

Preheat oven to 350 degrees. Line a baking sheet with parchment paper. In a heavy bottomed sauce pan, combine corn syrup, brown sugar and butter. Bring the mixture to a boil over medium heat while stirring constantly and let boil for 1 minute. Remove from heat and slowly stir in the flour. Then, add the almonds and vanilla extract to the mixture. Work quickly and drop the warm mixture by spoonfuls, about 3-4 inches apart onto the prepared baking sheet. Bake for 5 minutes until they have spread out and browned slightly. The cookies should be easily removed from the baking sheet but still a little pliable. If they are too soft, return to the oven for another 1-2 minutes. Remove from oven and cool for about 1 minute. Carefully remove from the parchment paper. The cookies will harden further as they cool. Store in an airtight container until ready to serve. These cookies are very fragile.

Chocolate Caramel Ganache Pops rolled in Cayenne Pumpkin Seed Brittle
Yields 24 pops

8 oz	semisweet chocolate chips
4 oz	unsweetened chocolate, chopped
1½ cups	heavy cream
2 Tbsp	butter
½ cup	sugar
⅛ tsp	fresh lemon juice
1 cup	cayenne pumpkin seed brittle, crushed
12	wooden skewers

Place the semisweet chocolate chips and unsweetened chocolate into a 4 quart bowl. Set aside. In a medium heavy sauce pan, combine the heavy cream and butter and warm over moderate heat and bring to a simmer. Set aside. In a medium sauce pan, combine the sugar and lemon juice. Whisk to combine so that the sugar resembles moist sand. Cook over high heat for 7-8 minutes stirring constantly. The sugar will become clear as it liquefies then it will brown as it caramelizes. Remove the saucepan from the heat. Carefully pour about ⅓ of the hot cream into the caramelized sugar. Whisk the caramel until it stops bubbling, then whisk in the remaining cream until the mixture is smooth. Immediately pour the hot caramel over the chopped chocolate and let stand for 5 minutes. Then, whisk the chocolate mixture until very smooth. Pour mixture into a sheet pan and smooth out with a rubber spatula. Refrigerate for 4 hours to overnight. Once completely chilled, use a melon baller and scrap the mixture to form small balls. Place pops on a clean baking sheet. Roll the balls in crushed cayenne pumpkin seed brittle. Return to the refrigerator until ready to serve. One hour before serving, place each ball on the end of a wooden skewer and freeze until serving.

CAYENNE PUMPKIN SEED BRITTLE
Yields 3 cups

1 cup	*sugar*
½ cup	*water*
1 pinch	*sea salt*
1 pinch	*cayenne pepper*
¾ cup	*raw, green pumpkin seeds (or 4 ounces), hulled*

Put a large sheet of parchment paper on a work surface and anchor the corners with pieces of masking tape. Set another sheet about the same size to the side. Bring the sugar, water, sea salt, and cayenne to a boil in a small heavy saucepan over moderate heat, stirring until the sugar is dissolved. Place a candy thermometer into the hot sugar and continue cooking the mixture without stirring. Wash down any sugar crystals on the side of the pan with a pastry brush dipped in cold water. Continue cooking until the syrup reaches 238 degrees on a candy thermometer (soft-ball stage). This will take about 10 minutes. Remove the syrup from the heat and stir in the pumpkin seeds with a wooden spoon. Continue stirring for 2-3 minutes until the syrup crystallizes. Return pan to moderate heat and cook for about 5 minutes. Stir constantly until sugar melts completely. The sugar will first dry out and become very grainy before it melts again. The sugar will turn a deep caramel color when the sugar has completely melted again. Carefully pour the hot sugar mixture onto the parchment paper and cover with another sheet of parchment. Remember to be careful because the caramel is very hot. Immediately roll out the caramel mixture (between the sheets of parchment) as thinly as possibly using a rolling pen. Remove the top sheet of the parchment and allow the brittle to cool completely. Peel the parchment paper from the bottom of the brittle and break into little pieces. If using the brittle for chocolate caramel ganache pops, place the brittle in a plastic Ziplock baggie and crush with the rolling pin.

NOTE: If you do not have a candy thermometer. Place a small glass of cool water near the stove. After about 10 minutes of cooking the sugar, place a small drop of the caramelized sugar in the water. If the sugar forms a small pliable ball, then you are at the soft ball stage.

Chocolate Dipped Strawberries
Yields 18 strawberries

18 lg	*strawberries, washed and dried well*
1 cup	*semisweet chocolate chips*

Line a baking sheet with parchment paper. Melt the chocolate in the top of a double boiler. When the chocolate is completely melted, carefully dip each strawberry ¾ way into the chocolate. Place on baking sheet to dry. Repeat the process until all of the strawberries are done. Refrigerate for about 1 hour to allow chocolate to set. This may be done up to 4 hours before serving.

Chocolate Martinis
Serves 8

2 Tbsp	*cocoa powder*
2 Tbsp	*sugar*
1 cup	*vanilla vodka*
½ cup	*chocolate liquor*
¼ cup	*chocolate syrup*
8	*chocolate swizzle sticks (store bought)*

Place 8 martini glasses in the freezer for 20 minutes. Mix cocoa powder and sugar together on a small plate. Fill another small plate with water. Dip the rim of the glasses into the water and then into the sugar cocoa mixture. In a blender, place the vodka, chocolate liquor and chocolate syrup together in a blender. Add ice to the top of the blender and blend until smooth. Pour mixture into prepared glasses and garnish with a chocolate swizzle stick.

Chocolate Pistachio Peppermint Bark

Serves 8

1 cup	semisweet chocolate chips, melted
¼ cup	pistachios, toasted and chopped
¼ cup	peppermint candies, crushed

Line a baking pan with parchment paper. Pour the melted chocolate onto the baking pan and spread using a spatula until the chocolate is a smooth thin layer. Allow the chocolate to cool for 5 minutes and then top with pistachios and peppermint candies. Refrigerate until ready to serve. Cut into peices and serve.

Chocolate Phyllo Purses

Yields 18 purses

18	Chocolate Truffles (store bought, or homemade) (see recipe)
1	box frozen phyllo dough
½ cup	butter (1 stick), melted
2 Tbsp	olive oil
1 cup	chocolate sauce
1	half gallon vanilla ice cream

Thaw and prepare the phyllo dough according to box instructions. Layer three pieces of phyllo dough, each brushed with ample amounts of butter. With a sharp knife, cut the phyllo into 3 x 3 inch squares. Place one truffle in the middle of each square. Fold the dough over and around the truffle. Where the dough comes together at the edges, twist the dough to seal. Place on a baking sheet and freeze for 3 hours or overnight. Preheat oven to 350 degrees. Bake in the oven until the phyllo dough is golden brown. Serve immediately on plates. Drizzle the chocolate sauce in a geometric design. Then, drizzle the olive oil in a similar fashion, hitting the blank areas of the plate, to create a stained glass look. Place three wrapped truffles on the plate and serve with vanilla ice cream.

CHOCOLATE TRUFFLES

Yields 24 truffles

12 oz	dark chocolate (60% cocoa or higher), chopped
4	egg yolks, beaten
¼ cup	heavy cream
½ cup	butter (1 stick), cut into small pieces
3 Tbsp	brandy or (Chambord, Framboise, Frangelico, Brandy, Amaretto or 1 teaspoon dried Lavender)
⅓ cup	unsweetened cocoa powder

Melt the chocolate in a glass bowl in the microwave on high in 30 second intervals. Be very careful not to get any water into the chocolate. In a heavy bottomed sauce pan, combine the egg yolks and heavy cream. Cook over medium-low heat, stirring constantly until thickened, about 7-10 minutes. Do not allow to boil. Remove from heat and slowly add the chocolate mixture while continuously stirring until well incorporated. Whisk in the pieces of butter one at a time until all of the butter is incorporated. At this time, add flavoring (or liquor) of choice. Cover with plastic wrap and refrigerate for at least 4 hours or overnight. Mixture will become very thick. When ready to assemble, place a piece of wax paper on a plate. Use a melon baller and scoop out about 2 teaspoons of mixture. Roll the mixture into a ball using your bands. It will help if you butter your hands. The heat from your hands will melt the chocolate very quickly. Once all the truffles are rolled, refrigerate for 30 minutes, and then roll in cocoa powder. Store the truffles in an airtight container. Freeze or refrigerate until ready to use.

Chocolate Wafer Cookies Dipped in White Chocolate

Yields 18 cookies

4 oz	white chocolate, chopped
18	Nabisco chocolate wafers

Place white chocolate in a glass bowl and melt in the microwave on high in 30 second intervals. Lay a piece of parchment paper on a baking sheet. Dip each cookie halfway into the white chocolate. Place on the parchment paper and cool. Refrigerate until ready to serve.

Cinnamon Maple Pecan Baked Apples

Serves 6

6 lg	Fuji apples (Granny smith or Macintosh)
½ cup	brown sugar
½ cup	maple syrup
2 Tbsp	ground cinnamon
½ cup	pecan pieces
¼ tsp	kosher salt
¼ cup	butter (½ stick) cut into 6 slices
¼ cup	water
1 pt	vanilla ice cream

Preheat the oven to 350 degrees. Wash apples and cut about ¼-½ of an inch off the bottom of each apple so that they can sit flat in baking dish. Remove the stem, core and seeds with an apple corer. In a medium sauce pan, warm the maple syrup and brown sugar until the brown sugar is completely dissolved. Add the cinnamon, pecans and salt to the mixture and stir until well incorporated. Remove from heat. Place the apples in a glass baking dish. Spoon the maple nut mixture into each of the apples. Place any additional topping in the pan around the apples. Top each of the apples with a slice of butter. Pour water into bottom of baking pan. Cover the apples with foil and bake for 30-45 minutes until apples are soft but not mushy. Serve warm with ice cream.

Citrus Fusion

Serves 6

6	lemon bars (use recipe or store bought)
1 cup	blood orange Anglaise
1 cup	meringue
2 cups	Grand Marnier ice cream, made into 6 large scoops
½ cup	lemon cello reduction
6	pistachio biscotti (may use store bought)
2	blood oranges, segmented and caramelized
½ cup	candied pistachios

To assemble dessert, use a large rectangular plate. Visualize, divide the plate into 2 parts. In one half, place one tablespoon of blood orange Anglaise on the plate and smear it with a spoon. Top the Anglaise with one lemon bar and a large dollop of meringue on top of the lemon bar. On the other half, place a scoop of Grand Marnier ice cream and top ice cream with biscotti. Use a hand torch and lightly toast the meringue. Drizzle the entire plate with the lemon cello reduction and garnish with the caramelized orange segments and candied pistachios.

PISTACHIO BISCOTTI

Yields 8-10 cookies

⅓ cup	pistachios, chopped
2 Tbsp	butter
1	egg
¼ cup	sugar
¼ tsp	vanilla extract
⅔ cup	all-purpose flour
¼ tsp	baking powder
⅛ tsp	salt

Preheat the oven to 350 degrees. Lay the pistachios on a cooking sheet in a single layer and bake for 10 minutes or until nuts are lightly toasted. Remove from the oven. In a medium mixing bowl, beat the butter and egg until light and fluffy. Add sugar and vanilla and mix until creamy. Add the flour, baking powder, and salt; mix the dough until smooth. Fold in the pistachios until evenly distributed. Place the dough on a lightly floured surface and form into a loaf about 6 inches long and 2 inches wide and 1 inch thick. Place on an ungreased cookie sheet and bake for 20 minutes or until the bottom is lightly browned. Remove from the oven and cool for 5 minutes. Slice the loaf into approximately ½ inch thick pieces. Put the cookies back on the cookie sheet and bake for 5-10 minutes. Turn the cookies over and bake for another 5-10 minutes. Biscotti should be hard and golden on the outside. Store the cookies in an airtight container until ready to use.

BLOOD ORANGE ANGLAISE

Yields 1 cup

2	egg yolks
1 Tbsp	sugar
½ cup	heavy cream
1 Tbsp	blood orange juice

In a mixing bowl, combine the egg yolks and sugar. With a hand mixer, beat until the mixture is thick and light. In a heavy sauce pan, heat the heavy cream until scalded. With the mixer running on low, very gradually pour the scalded milk into the egg yolk mixture. Add in the blood orange juice and mix until well incorporated. Pour the mixture back into the sauce pan. Heat it slowly, stirring constantly, until thickened enough to coat the back of a wooden spoon. Remove from heat and stir until the sauce cools.

GRAND MARNIER ICE CREAM

Yields 2 cups

1 pt	high-quality vanilla ice cream
¼ cup	Grand Marnier

At least 6 hours before serving, remove the ice cream from the freezer and scoop into a bowl. Allow to soften slightly. Stir in Grand Marnier into the ice cream and place the mixture back into the freezer as quickly as possible. Try not to let the ice cream thaw too much.

LEMONCELLO REDUCTION

Yields 2 cups

1 cup	high-quality lemon cello
½ cup	sugar
½ cup	water
1	lemon, cut in half

Put all the ingredients in a medium sauce pan. Bring the mixture to a boil over high heat and boil for 2-3 minutes. Remove from the heat and remove lemon halves and refrigerate until ready to serve.

MERINGUE

Yields 1 cup

6	egg whites
3 Tbsp	sugar

In a medium mixing bowl, beat the egg whites until frothy. Add the sugar and continue beating until stiff peaks form.

CARAMELIZED BLOOD ORANGE SEGMENTS

Serves 8

6	blood oranges, peeled and segmented
6 Tbsp	butter
3 Tbsp	brown sugar

Melt the butter in a heavy bottomed skillet or sauce pan over medium heat. Add in the brown sugar and the blood orange segments. Stir until the sugar is dissolved and the mixture begins to bubble. Reduce the heat to low and stir occasionally for about 5 minutes. The segments will become tender and the caramel sauce will have a syrupy consistency. Remove from heat and cool to room temperature.

CANDIED PISTACHIOS

Yields 1 cup

1 cup	pistachios
¼ cup	sugar
¼ cup	water

Preheat oven to 350 degrees. In a small saucepan, bring water and sugar to a boil over medium heat. Add pistachios and cook for 5 minutes. Pour mixture onto baking sheet and bake for 5-10 minutes until lightly browned. Remove from oven and sprinkle with additional granulated sugar. Allow to dry at room temperature and store at room temperature until ready to use.

Creamy Pralines

Yields 20 cookies

½ cup	white sugar
½ cup	brown sugar
¾ cup	heavy cream
1 cup	pecans
3 Tbsp	butter
2 Tbsp	light corn syrup

In a medium, heavy bottomed saucepan heat the sugar, brown sugar and cream together. Bring the mixture to a boil over high heat. Boil until the mixture is a golden caramel color. Add the pecans, butter and corn syrup. Stir well. Remove from the heat and vigorously whisk the mixture until it loses its gloss and cools slightly. Using a tablespoon, drop the mixture onto wax (or parchment paper). Allow the mixture to cool and dry. Store the pralines in an airtight container, until ready to use. If the mixture gets too hard, return to the stove top and warm (or add a small amount of additional cream).

Crème Bruleé with Caramelized Strawberries

Serves 6

1½	cups heavy cream
1½	cups whole milk
6 lg	egg yolks
½ cup	sugar
½ tsp	vanilla extract
1 cup	light brown sugar
1 pt	strawberries, sliced
¼ cup	sugar

Preheat the oven to 325 degrees. In a medium, heavy bottom sauce pan, heat the heavy cream and whole milk over medium heat until scalded (heat to just before boiling). In a separate bowl, beat the egg yolks and ½ cup sugar with an electric mixer until pale yellow. Add the vanilla extract to the milk mixture. Carefully pour the hot milk mixture into the eggs yolks in a very slow steady stream. Stir constantly until all the milk is incorporated into the yolk mixture. This is one of the most important steps to making crème bruleé. Once the batter is well incorporated, pour into a 1½ quart ceramic casserole dish (or into 6 small ceramic ramekins). Place the ceramic dishes onto a baking pan at least 2 inches deep. Fill the baking pan half way with water. Place the baking pan with crème brulee in the oven and bake for 1-1½ hours until the crème bruleé is set. Using a thin, rounded end knife, insert the knife into the crème bruleé. If the knife comes out clean, the crème bruleé is ready to remove from the oven. If not, return to the oven and check every 15 minutes until set. Remove the crème bruleé from the water bath and cool at room temperature for at least 2 hours. Refrigerate overnight. When ready to serve, preheat the oven on broil. Top the crème bruleés with a thin layer of brown sugar. Place the crème bruleés in a baking dish and place under the broiler. Watch carefully because the sugar will burn very easily. Once the sugar starts to bubble, remove from the oven and cool for 5-10 minutes before serving. You may also use a kitchen torch to caramelize the brown sugar. Remove the green tops from the strawberries and slice in half. Toss the strawberries with ¼ cup sugar. Place the strawberries on top of the crème bruleé just before serving.

Crepes Suzette

Serves 8

24	dessert crepes
2 cups	butter (4 sticks)
1 cup	sugar
2 lg	oranges, juiced
½ cup	brandy or cognac
¼ cup	orange flavored liqueur, such as Grand Marnier

In a large, heavy bottomed skillet over medium heat, melt the butter. Add sugar and continue stirring until dissolved. Add juice of orange and stir. Place each crepe in the pan and dredge through the mixture. Fold the crepe using 2 spoons into quarters. Continue until all the crepes are in the pan. As you are folding the crepes, shingle them on top of each other so they will all fit in the pan. Turn the heat to high and bring the mixture to a vigorous boil. Add the brandy and orange liqueur. Pull the pan back slightly from the flame and allow the pan to ignite (or ignite with a lighter). Turn off the heat and gently shake the pan until the flame subsides. Serve hot.

DESSERT CREPES
Yields 24 crepes

¾ cup	milk
1 Tbsp	sugar
¾ cup	cold water
2 Tbsp	brandy or cognac
3	egg yolks
2 cups	flour, sifted
5 Tbsp	butter, melted
¼ cup	vegetable oil

Mix all of the ingredients together in an electric blender. Blend for 1 minute at highest speed. Place the batter in the refrigerator for 2-4 hours. While waiting for batter to chill, cut 24 squares of wax paper about 6 x 6 to use for stacking the crepes. When ready to cook crepes, place 1 teaspoon of vegetable oil in a crepe skillet (or small omelet pan) and heat on medium-high heat for 1 minute. Pour a scant ¼ cup of batter into the heated, oiled crepe pan and twirl the pan until the batter looks like a thin pancake. Cook the crepe until it is lightly browned on the underside of the crepe. Carefully turn the crepe over and brown on the back side. Gently remove the crepe from the pan using a rubber spatula and place onto a plate. Place a piece of wax paper on top of crepe and continue this process until all the crepes are cooked. Stacking the crepes with wax paper keeps them from sticking to each other and makes for easy storage.

NOTE: If you have never made crepes before, do not despair. It can be a little tricky but it is worth the effort. This is a process that takes a little patience and sometimes a few tries to get it right. If the first couple of crepes do not work, add a little flour to the mixture and try again. You will eventually get the hang of it.

Croquembouche
Serves 20

Pastry Cream:

⅔ cup	sugar
⅓ cup	all-purpose flour
2 cups	milk
4 lg	egg yolks

Cream Puff:

¼ cup	water
¼ cup	milk
¼ cup	butter (½ stick)
2 Tbsp	sugar
¾ cup	all-purpose flour (plus 2 tablespoons extra)
4 lg	eggs

Caramel Sugar:

2½ cups	sugar
⅔ cup	water

Pastry Cream:
In a medium, heavy bottomed sauce pan, whisk together sugar and flour. Gradually whisk in milk and then the egg yolks. Cook over medium heat while whisking constantly until thickens and boils, about 10 minutes. Remove from heat. Transfer to a bowl, and press plastic wrap on top of the surface of the cream to prevent a skin from forming. Refrigerate pastry cream until cold and firm, about 3 hours.

Cream Puffs:
Preheat oven to 375 degrees. Line 2 baking sheets with parchment paper. In a medium, heavy bottomed sauce pan, combine water, milk, butter and sugar. Heat over medium heat and bring to a boil, whisking constantly until sugar dissolves and butter melts. Remove from heat. Add flour and whisk until smooth and blended (dough will form into a ball). Stir over low heat until dough leaves a film on the pan bottom, about 2 minutes. Transfer the dough to a large mixing bowl. Allow the dough to cool for about 7-8 minutes. Using an electric mixer, beat in eggs, one at a time. Drop batter by teaspoon fulls onto prepared baking sheets (around 1 tablespoon each). Using moistened finger tips, smooth away pointed tips on the batter mounds. Bake the puffs at 375 degrees for 20 minutes. Reduce heat to 350 degrees and continue to bake until puffs are firm and beginning to crack and dry on top, about 20 minutes longer. Remove from oven and use

a small knife to poke a hole inside of each puff, near the bottom to allow steam to escape. Allow to cool completely. Spoon the pastry cream into a pastry bag, with a small tip. Pipe the filling into each puff. Refrigerate until ready to use.

NOTE: You may buy cream puffs from a French bakery if you prefer.

Caramel Sugar:
Prepare an ice bath in a medium mixing bowl by filling it with ice and water to about ½ full. In a medium, heavy bottomed saucepan, heat the sugar and water over medium heat, until sugar is dissolved. Bring to a boil and continue heating until sugar is golden in color. Place pan of caramel in ice bath to stop the cooking process.

Assembly:
Use a tray or round board covered in foil, at least 12-14 inches in diameter. Dip the cream puffs one at a time into slightly cooled caramel. Place each one on a tray/board in a circle touching each other. Fill in center of circle with more cream puffs. This should take about 18-24 puffs. Begin a second row on top of the first, slightly inside the other circle to eventually create a tower of puffs. When finished drizzle remaining caramel all over the tower, creating strings of sugar.

NOTE: If very humid outside the sugar will not harden and strings will be hard to create, however it will still taste fantastic.

Crumb Crust Apple Pie
Serves 8

Crust:
1	9 inch deep dish frozen pie crust

Filling:
6 med	granny smith apples, peeled and thinly sliced
¾ cup	sugar
2 Tbsp	flour
1 tsp	cinnamon
1 Tbsp	lemon juice
3 Tbsp	butter, cut into small pieces

Topping:
½ cup	sugar
½ cup	flour
½ cup	cold butter (1 sticks)

Preheat the oven to 375 degrees. Line a baking sheet with aluminum foil. Place the sliced apples in a mixing bowl with sugar, flour, cinnamon, and lemon juice. Toss until well combined. Place the apples and any liquid in the bowl into the unbaked pie crust. The apples should be higher than the crust. Top the apples with the pieces of butter. Cover the pie with foil and bake for 30 minutes on a baking sheet. To make the crumb crust, combine sugar and flour in food processor and mix well. Add butter and pulse until just mixed and very crumbly. Remove the pie from the oven, remove the foil, and sprinkle the topping over the apples. Return the pie to the oven and bake for an additional 30-40 minutes or until golden brown on top. Serve warm with vanilla ice cream.

NOTE: This is a messy pie, but well worth the mess. The topping will melt over the edges of the pie and onto the baking sheet. The foil lining helps for a quick clean up.

Dark and White Chocolate Mousse in Champagne Flutes
Serves 8

White Chocolate Mousse:
½ lb	baking white chocolate or white chocolate chips
1 Tbsp	butter
1 Tbsp	sugar
3	egg yolks
3	egg whites
½ cup	heavy cream

Place chocolate in the top of double boiler with the butter. Put over boiling water and stir until chocolate is completely melted. Remove from heat and set aside. In a separate mixing bowl, beat the sugar with the egg yolks until the mixture is light and creamy. In a separate bowl, beat the egg whites until stiff peaks form. Gently fold the egg whites into the egg yolks. Gently fold the chocolate and butter mixture into the egg mixture. Beat cream until stiff and fold into the chocolate mixture. Chill for 2-3 hours or overnight.

Dark Chocolate Mouse:

½ lb	dark bittersweet chocolate (60% cocoa)
1 Tbsp	butter
1 Tbsp	sugar
3	egg yolks
3	egg whites
½ cup	heavy cream

Follow the same instructions as for the white chocolate mousse.

Assembly

1 cup	heavy cream, whipped; for garnish
1 cup	chocolate shavings, for garnish

To assemble, spoon ¼ cup of white chocolate mousse into champagne flute. Top with ¼ cup of dark chocolate mousse. Top with ¼ whipped cream and chocolate shavings. Refrigerate until ready to use.

Dark Chocolate Cheesecake Tarts with Chocolate Crust and Chocolate Ganache Topping

Yields 24 tartlets

Crust:

24	chocolate Nabisco wafer cookies
1 Tbsp	sugar
¼ cup	butter (½ stick) melted

Filling:

9 oz	bittersweet chocolate (dark chocolate 70% cocoa), chopped
1 lb	cream cheese, softened
1¼ cups	sugar
¼ cup	unsweetened cocoa powder
4 lg	eggs

Ganache:

¾ cup	heavy cream
6 oz	high quality bittersweet chocolate, chopped
1 Tbsp	sugar

Crust:

Preheat oven to 350 degrees. Spray 1½"-2" metal tartlet shells with food release spray or Pam. Place chocolate wafer cookies in food processor and pulse until finely ground. Add the sugar and butter and process until incorporated. Press the crumbs evenly onto the bottom and sides of the tartlet shells. Bake about 5 minutes. Remove from the oven and cool.

Filling:

Using a double boiler or a metal bowl on top of a pot of boiling water, stir chopped chocolate until melted and smooth. Remove bowl from heat. Then, in a food processor, blend the cream cheese, sugar, and cocoa powder until smooth. Add the eggs, one at a time and pulse after each addition. Pour the melted chocolate into the cream cheese mixture and mix. Spoon the mixture into the prepared crusts until about ¾ full. Bake at 350 degrees for 20-30 minutes until set. Remove tarts from shell and refrigerate overnight. When ready to serve, top with ganache.

Ganache:

Place cream, chocolate and sugar in a medium, heavy bottomed sauce pan over low heat and stir until chocolate is melted and smooth. Remove from heat and allow to cool for about 10 minutes. Drizzle on tops of tarts and serve.

NOTE: If you want to make a large cheesecake, use a 9½" spring-form pan and bake for additional 10-15 minutes.

Dark Chocolate Pot de Crème with Espresso Cream

Serving Size: 8

12 oz.	*dark semisweet chocolate, chopped into pieces*
12	*eggs*
½ cup	*sugar*
2 Tbsp	*dark rum*
½ cup	*espresso cream*
8	*chocolate covered espresso beans, for garnish*

Melt chocolate in a metal bowl over hot boiling water. Stir until smooth. Remove the boil from heat and let cool slightly. In the same hot boiling water, carefully place the eggs in the water for 1 minute, using a slotted spoon. This is to kill the bacteria on the outside of the egg because the eggs are used raw in this recipe. Remove the eggs from the water and set aside to cool. Then, separate the eggs yolks and whites. In a mixing bowl, beat egg yolks with sugar until pale yellow. Add the rum and set aside. In another mixing bowl, beat egg whites until stiff. Stir the egg yolks and rum into the warm chocolate mixture. Fold in egg whites. Spoon the mixture into ceramic 4 ounce ramekins. Refrigerate for 4 hours or overnight. When ready to serve, top each one with 1 tablespoon of espresso cream and one chocolate covered espresso bean.

ESPRESSO CREAM

Yield: 2 cups

1 cup	*heavy cream*
1 tsp	*instant espresso powder*
1 Tbsp	*water*
3 Tbsp	*sugar*

NOTE: May use brewed espresso instead of powder and water.

Beat the cream in a mixing bowl until still. In a small bowl, stir together the espresso powder, water and sugar until dissolved. Fold liquid into the cream and refrigerate until ready to use.

Fresh Fruit Sorbets Served in Hollowed Out Fruits

Serves 8

1 lg	*lime*
1 lg	*lemon*
1 lg	*orange*
1 lg	*mango*
4 lg	*strawberries*
1 cup	*lemon sorbet (store bought)*
1 cup	*lime sorbet (store bought)*
1 cup	*mango sorbet (store bought)*
1 cup	*strawberry sorbet (store bought)*
1 cup	*orange sorbet (store bought)*

Cut the lemon, lime and orange in halve. Use a grapefruit spoon or a small paring knife and remove the flesh of the fruits. Be careful not to cut the rind. You will be left with citrus cups. Cut the mango in half and carefully remove the seed. Scoop out about ½ of the flesh of the mango, making a small hole in the center. Cut the strawberries in halve and remove the stem. Place all the fruits on a serving tray and place in freezer for at least 2 hours. When ready to serve, remove the fruits from the freezer and scoop a small amount of similar sorbet into the fruit cups. For instance, lemon sorbet into the lemon cups. Return fruits filled with sorbet to freezer for at least 30 minutes before serving. Serve on a tray with crushed ice.

Fresh Pumpkin Pie

Serves 10

4 cups	fresh pumpkin (1 pie pumpkin)
¾ cup	milk
2 lg	eggs
½ cup	brown sugar
½ tsp	ground cinnamon
½ tsp	ground ginger
⅛ tsp	ground nutmeg
⅛ tsp	ground cloves
1 Tbsp	dark molasses
2 Tbsp	butter, melted
1	9 inch frozen pie crust
1 cup	heavy cream, chilled

Preheat the oven to 375 degrees. Cut the pumpkin in half and scoop the seeds out of both sides. Place each half of the pumpkin on a baking sheet open side down. Bake in oven until the pumpkin is soft-about 45 minutes to 1 hour. Remove from the oven and cool for 10 minutes. Turn the pumpkin halves over and scoop the pulp away from the skin. Discard the skin and put the pumpkin pulp in a blender or food processor, then blend until smooth. Heat the milk in sauce pan over medium heat until it just starts to bubble around the edges. Remove from heat. Beat eggs in large bowl until frothy. Add scalded milk to the eggs and stir constantly. Add pumpkin puree, brown sugar, molasses and butter, cinnamon, ginger, nutmeg, cloves and stir until thoroughly blended. Pour filling in to prepared crust, and bake until the center is firm, about 45 minutes. Cool completely on wire rack. When ready to serve, beat chilled cream with mixer until stiff peaks form. Spoon on top of pie and serve.

Frozen Tiramisu

Serves 12

32	hard ladyfingers
½ cup	brewed coffee
¼ cup	dark rum
1 pt	chocolate gelato (may use chocolate ice cream)
2 qt	coffee ice cream
8 oz	mascarpone cheese
4 oz	cream cheese
3 Tbsp	Kahlua
1 Tbsp	sugar
½ cup	heavy cream, whipped
4 oz	dark chocolate (at least 60%), grated
2 Tbsp	unsweetened cocoa powder
2 Tbsp	powdered sugar
½ cup	maraschino cherries, diced

Line a 2 quart loaf pan (or a 2 quart glass baking dish) with two long pieces of plastic wrap. Make sure that you cover the entire inside of the pan and leave extra to hang over the edges about 4 inches. Line the pan, on top of the plastic, with the lady fingers. Cover both the bottom and sides. On the bottom, line the lady fingers long wise and on the sides, stand them up. Do not overlap. Mix the coffee and the rum together and drizzle over the lady fingers. Remove the chocolate gelato from the freezer and soften slightly. Spread the chocolate gelato over the lady fingers with a spatula. Return to freezer for 30 minutes. Remove the coffee ice cream from the freezer and soften. Spread the coffee ice cream over the gelato. Smooth the ice cream out evenly. Cover with plastic wrap and place pan in the freezer for 2 hours. In a medium mixing bowl, whip the mascarpone cheese with the cream cheese using an electric mixer. Add Kahlua and the sugar. In a separate bowl, whip the cream until stiff. Fold the whipped cream into the mascarpone mixture. Remove pan from freezer. Remove plastic and spoon mixture on top of the coffee ice cream. Sprinkle with chopped dark chocolate. Return to freezer for 30 minutes-1 hour or until ready to serve. Remove from freezer and turn tiramisu onto a serving platter. Remove the plastic and top with cocoa powder and powdered sugar. Slice and serve with additional whipped cream, if desired. Garnish with maraschino cherries.

Grand Marnier Soufflé
Serves 6

7	egg whites
¾ cup	sugar
2 cups	milk
⅓ cup	flour
4 Tbsp	butter, melted
5	egg yolks
2 oz	Grand Marnier

Grease the inside of ceramic 2 quart soufflé dish with butter and sprinkle with sugar. Preheat the oven to 400 degrees. In a mixing bowl, beat the egg whites until soft peaks. Add the sugar and continue to beat till stiff peaks form. Set aside. Heat the milk in a heavy sauce pan over medium heat. In a small bowl, mix melted butter with the flour and stir into hot milk, blend well. Continue cooking and stirring over medium heat until a thick creamy consistency is reached. Remove from the heat and stir in Grand Marnier. In a mixing bowl, beat the egg yolks until pale yellow in color and add to milk mixture, continually stirring. Gently fold beaten egg whites into the mixture. Pour into a prepared soufflé dish. Bake at 400 degrees for 20-25 minutes. Serve immediately with Grand Marnier Crème Anglaise (see recipe below).

GRAND MARNIER CREAM ANGLAISE
Yields 1 quart

3	egg yolks
¼ cup	sugar
1 cup	heavy cream
2 Tbsp	Grand Marnier

Combine the egg yolks and sugar in a medium mixing bowl. Beat the mixture with a hand mixer until the batter is thick and light. Place the cream in a medium sauce pan and heat until scalded or just before boiling. With the mixer running on low, very gradually pour the scaled cream into the egg yolk mixture. Pour the mixture back into the saucepan and heat it slowly, stirring constantly until thickened enough to coat the back of a wooden spoon. Be careful to not boil the mixture—it will curdle. Add the Grand Marnier. Remove from heat and stir until cooled slightly.

Iced Lemon Mousse with Pistachios
Serves 10

2	envelopes unflavored gelatin
½ cup	cold water
12	eggs yolks
2½ cups	sugar
1½ cups	lemon juice
⅓ cup	lemon zest
14	egg whites
¼ tsp	salt
¼ tsp	cream of tartar
¼ cup	sugar
3 cups	heavy cream
1 cup	pistachios, chopped and roasted
1 cup	vegetable oil

Take a piece of foil, approximately 30 inches long and fold it to be approximately 5 inches wide. Brush foil strip on one side with vegetable oil. Place the foil piece around the outside of the ceramic dish allowing at least 2 inches above the rim. Secure foil with a large rubber band. In a small bowl, sprinkle the gelatin over the cold water and let soften for 10 minutes. In a large metal mixing bowl, place the egg yolks, sugar, lemon juice, and lemon zest. Place the bowl over a pot of boiling water. With an electric hand mixer, beat the egg mixture until thickened, about 10 minutes. Remove from heat. Place the bowl of gelatin over the pan of hot water and stir the mixture until the gelatin is dissolved. Pour the gelatin mixture into the egg yolk mixture, stirring until it is well mixed. Make an ice bath using a large mixing bowl filled with ice and water. Set the bowl of lemon mixture in the ice bath and stir until it is just cool but not set. In a separate bowl, beat the egg whites with the salt until frothy. Add the cream of tartar and beat until they hold soft peaks. Add sugar and beat until the whites hold stiff peaks. In a separate bowl, beat heavy cream until stiff. Fold the whipped cream and egg whites into the lemon mixture. Thoroughly, but gently, mix together and spoon the mixture into the prepared soufflé dish. Smooth the top and chill for at least 4 hours or overnight. When ready to serve remove the foil collar, and press pistachios into the side of the soufflé that is above the dish rim. Garnish with additional whipped cream piped on the top.

Lemon Bars with Lemon Zest

Serves 16 Squares

Crust:
1 cup	flour
¼ cup	powdered sugar
½ cup	butter (1 stick), melted

Filling:
2	eggs, beaten
2 tsp	baking powder
1 cup	sugar
2 Tbsp	flour
2 Tbsp	lemon juice
1 tsp	lemon zest

Preheat the oven to 350 degrees. In a mixing bowl, stir together flour, powdered sugar and melted butter. Press mixture into 9" square pan. Use a metal spatula and press crust down so that it is evenly distributed. Bake crust 15 minutes until lightly browned. Remove from oven and cool for 5 minutes. In a mixing bowl, stir together eggs, baking powder, granulated sugar, and flour. After well mixed, pour in the lemon juice and zest. Pour over the crust and return to oven for 20-25 minutes until lightly browned on top. Remove from oven and cool. Cut into 2 x 2 inch squares.

Lemon Blueberry Bars with Lemon Zest Glaze

Serves 16 squares

Crust:
1	box yellow cake mix
¼ cup	butter (½ stick)
2	eggs

Filling:
1 cup	frozen blueberries, thawed
4	eggs
16 oz	cream cheese, softened
5 cups	powdered sugar
½ Tbsp	lemon zest
½ tsp	lemon juice
1 cup	lemon zest glaze

Preheat oven to 350 degrees.

Crust:
Grease a 15 x 10 glass baking dish with butter. In a large mixing bowl, beat together cake mix, butter and eggs with electric beater until crumbly.

Filling:
Place blueberries in a blender and blend until smooth. Put blueberry puree in a medium sauce pan and bring to a boil over medium heat. Continue boiling until reduced in half.
In a mixing bowl combine eggs, cream cheese, powdered sugar, lemon zest and lemon juice. Beat until blended. Pour mixture over the crust. Drizzle blueberry puree over the filling in straight lines about 2 inches apart along the length of the pan. Drag a toothpick through the lines in opposite directions every 2 inches. The end result will be a slight rippled look. Bake 20-30 minutes until top is light brown. Remove from oven and let cool completely. Spread the lemon glaze over the top. Cut into 2 x 2 inch squares.

LEMON ZEST GLAZE

Yields 2 cups

1 cup	*sugar*
½ cup	*buttermilk*
½ cup	*butter (1 stick)*
3 Tbsp	*lemon zest*

Combine all ingredients in a heavy bottomed saucepan. Cook over medium heat for 5-7 minutes. Remove from heat and cool completely.

Lime Zest Sand Tarts

Yields 4-5 dozen

1 cup	*butter (2 sticks)*
⅓ cup	*sugar*
2½ tsp	*vanilla extract*
2 tsp	*water*
2 cups	*flour*
1 cup	*pecans, finely minced*
2 Tbsp	*lime zest*
1 cup	*powdered sugar, sifted*

In a medium mixing bowl, blend butter and sugar with a hand mixer. Add vanilla extract and the water, and then add the flour, pecans and lime zest. Blend well. Refrigerate batter for 1 hour. Preheat the oven to 325 degrees. Roll the batter into small balls about 1" in diameter and placed on an ungreased cookie sheet. Bake the cookies for 15-20 minutes, until edges are pale brown. Cool slightly. While cookies are still warm, roll them in powdered sugar.

Mandarin Orange Mousse

Serves 12

2 Tbsp	*gelatin powder*
½ cup	*water*
2 cups	*sugar*
4	*egg yolks*
2 cups	*orange juice*
3 Tbsp	*lemon juice*
2 cups	*heavy cream*
1 cup	*canned mandarin oranges, drained*
4	*whole tangerines, cut into quarters*
1	*bunch fresh mint*

Create an ice bath by filling large mixing bowl half full with ice and water. In a small bowl, place the gelatin and water. Allow the gelatin to soften for 5 minutes. Combine the sugar, egg yolks and orange juice in a medium sauce pan over low heat. Whisk continuously until the mixture is steaming and slightly thickened. Do not allow to come to a boil. Once the mixture is thickened, remove from heat. Add the gelatin mixture and lemon juice. Transfer the mixture to a mixing bowl and place bowl into ice bath. Cool the mixture, stirring occasionally until it becomes syrupy. Beat the heavy cream until stiff peaks. Gently fold the whipped cream into the custard mix. Place the mandarin orange segments in the bottom of a Bundt pan. Pour the custard over the oranges. Refrigerate for at least 4 hours or overnight. When ready to serve, fill a sink with about 2" of very hot water. Place the Bundt pan into the hot water for up to one minute to loosen the mold. Shake the pan gently to see if the gelatin has released from the sides. Place a serving tray over the Bundt pan and turn upside down. The mold should release from the pan onto the plate. Garnish the mold with tangerine pieces and fresh mint.

Miss Judy's Banana Puddin' Shots

Serves 12

5 lg	egg yolks
½ cup	sugar
2 cups	heavy cream
½ Tbsp	vanilla extract
20	vanilla wafer cookies
1 Tbsp	sugar
1 Tbsp	butter, cold
2 lg	ripe bananas, peeled and sliced
1	egg white
1 Tbsp	sugar

In a medium mixing bowl, beat the egg yolks and sugar with an electric mixer until thick and light in color. Heat the heavy cream in a medium, heavy bottomed sauce pan over medium heat until scalded or just before boiling. Add the scalded cream, very slowly, to the egg mixture and stir constantly until all the cream is incorporated. Return the mixture to the pot and heat while continuously stirring and cook the custard until it coats the back of a spoon. This will take 8-10 minutes. When thick, remove from the heat and add the vanilla extract. Stir for 1 minute off of the fire. Place the custard in a clean bowl and set aside to cool. Place a piece of plastic wrap directly on top of custard and refrigerate until ready to use. This will keep a film from developing on top of custard. While the pudding sets, preheat the oven to 350 degrees. In a food processor, place the vanilla wafers, sugar and butter and pulse until the mixture just comes together and is crumbly. Place crumbs on a baking sheet and bake for 3-5 minutes until golden brown. Remove from oven and cool completely. When ready to assemble, beat egg whites until soft peaks form. Add sugar and continue beating until stiff peaks and glossy, about 5 minutes. Place one slice of banana on the bottom of the shot glass. Top with one tablespoon of custard and a little of the crumble. Repeat until the shot glass is full. Spoon one tablespoon of the meringue on top of the glass. Use a hand torch and slightly brown the meringue. Garnish with fresh mint.

Multi-Berry Shortcake

Serves 8

8	cream scones (recipe in bread section)
4 cups	heavy cream
½ cup	sugar
1 pt	blueberries, washed and dried
1 pt	raspberries, washed and dried
1 pt	strawberries, sliced, washed and dried
1 pt	blackberries, washed and dried

Whip the heavy cream until stiff, and then add sugar. Cut the scones in half lengthwise. Place the bottom half of the scone on a plate, then spoon about 4 tablespoons of the whipped cream on top of scone. Garnish with 1 cup mixed berries. Place the scone top over the berries and top with additional whipped cream.

Old Fashioned Butter Toffee with Almonds

Yields 2 quarts

2 cups	butter (4 sticks)
2 cups	sugar
1 cup	whole almonds, salted
1 lb	semisweet chocolate chips

In a medium, heavy bottom skillet, heat the butter and sugar over medium high heat stirring constantly until melted. Continue stirring until the mixture begins to caramelize. Add the almonds and continue stirring; cook until the mixture turns a medium deep brown caramel color. Remove from heat and pour into a baking pan. Allow the mixture to harden in the pan at room temperature. Melt the chocolate chips in a glass bowl in the microwave on high in 30 seconds intervals until melted. Once the chocolate is melted, pour over the hardened candy and cool until chocolate is hardened. Wrap in plastic wrap until ready to use. When ready, use a knife and break the toffee into bit size pieces. Keep the toffee in air tight container for up to three weeks.

Peach Tarte Tatin
Serves 8

1	sheet refrigerated pie crust

Tarte Tatin:

½ cup	sugar
2 tsp	light corn syrup
1 tsp	brown sugar
3 Tbsp	water
2 Tbsp	butter, melted
1 tsp	fresh squeezed lemon juice
1 lb	frozen unsweetened peach slices

Preheat the oven to 375 degrees. In a medium oven safe, cast iron skillet, combine the sugar, corn syrup, brown sugar and water. Cook over medium heat until sugar dissolves. Increase heat and bring to a boil. Do not stir. Syrup will turn to dark amber color. Occasionally use a wet pastry brush to remove sugar from sides of skillet. This will take about 5-7 minutes. Remove skillet from fire. Add butter and lemon juice to syrup and stir. Add peaches to syrup. Arrange peach slices around the pan in a circle covering the bottom of the pan. Place pie dough on top of peaches and press dough lightly against peaches. Push the dough down around the peaches in the pan. Place in oven and bake until it is golden brown, or about 20 minutes. Remove from oven and use a knife to loosen the pastry from the pan. Let cool for 5-10 minutes. Place large plate or platter over skillet. Be sure to use oven mitts or towels. Invert pan onto plate and allow tarte to settle onto the platter. Remove the skillet very carefully. Replace peaches that may have moved or been stuck to bottom of skillet. Serve with Romanoff sauce or ice cream.

Pecan Tassies with Bourbon Clotted Cream
Yields 24 tartlets

24	tartlet shells, unbaked (use tartlet dough recipe)
1 cup	brown sugar
½ cup	sugar
1½ Tbsp	flour
2	eggs
3 Tbsp	milk
1 tsp	vanilla extract
½ cup	butter, melted
1 cup	pecans, chopped

Preheat oven to 375 degrees. In a medium mixing bowl, mix the brown sugar, white sugar and flour. Add eggs, milk, vanilla extract and melted butter to the mixture; beat until well mixed. Stir in the pecans. Pour the pie filling in the unbaked tartlet shells. Bake for about 15 minutes or until set. When the tartlets are done cooking, remove from the heat and let cool completely. Before serving, top with the Bourbon Clotted Cream (see recipe below).

BOURBON CLOTTED CREAM
Yields 2 cups

1 cup	heavy cream
⅛ cup	sugar
⅛ cup	bourbon

In a metal bowl, whip the heavy cream. When soft peaks form, add sugar and bourbon. Continue beating until very stiff, then beat a little longer until cream just starts to get clumpy.

Quattro Apple

Serves 8

8	warm granny smith apple galettes
2 cups	sauterne poached macintosh apples
2 cups	calvados cream caramel sauce
4 cups	apple basil ginger granita
8	cinnamon sugar cookies
	Fresh Mint

Drizzle a dinner plate with the caramel sauce. Place a warm apple galette in the middle of the plate. Drizzle more caramel sauce over the tart. Spoon poached apples on top of tart. Serve in a shot glass on the side, with cinnamon sugar cookies.

WARM GRANNY SMITH APPLE GALETTE

Serves 8

4	boxes refrigerated pie dough
3 lg	granny smith apples, peeled, cored, and thinly sliced
½ cup	sugar
1 tsp	cinnamon
1 Tbsp	flour
1 Tbsp	lemon juice

Preheat oven to 350 degrees. Unroll pie dough and cut into 6 inch round pieces. Press the dough pieces into 4 inch fluted tart shell pans. Place the tartlet shells on a baking sheet. Place the apple slices, sugar, cinnamon, flour and lemon juice in a large mixing bowl. Toss to combine. Spoon the apple mixture into shells. Bake until apples are tender and crust is golden brown, about 30-40 minutes.

SAUTERNE POACHED MACINTOSH APPLES

Yields 2 cups

2	Macintosh (or other hard tart apple) peeled and cut into wedges
1 cup	sauterne wine
½ cup	water
1 cup	sugar

Bring wine, water, and sugar to a boil in a medium saucepan. Add the apple wedges and boil for 5 minutes. Remove from the heat and let apples sit in wine for 30 minutes. Remove apples from liquid with a slotted spoon.

CALVADOS CREAM CARAMEL SAUCE

Yields 3 cups

1½ cups	granulated sugar
½ cup	water
1 cup	heavy cream
2 Tbsp	Calvados (or other apple liqueur)

In a medium, heavy bottomed saucepan, stir together sugar and water. Cook over medium heat until the sugar is completely dissolved. Continue cooking for about 15 minutes until the sugar begins to change to a caramel color. Do not stir and occasionally brush down the sides of the pot with a pastry brush dipped in cold water. After the caramel becomes golden brown, remove the pan from the heat. Carefully add a small amount of the cream, and stir. Be careful as the caramel will produce a lot of steam. Then, stir in the rest of the cream. Remove from heat and add Calvados. Cool caramel sauce to room temperature.

APPLE BASIL GINGER GRANITA

Yields 4½ cups

½ cup	sugar
1 Tbsp	fresh basil, finely chopped
½ tsp	ginger powder
4 cups	apple juice

Pulse together the sugar, basil and ginger powder in a blender or food processor until the sugar is bright green. Stir in the apple juice until the sugar is dissolved. Pour mixture into medium glass baking pan. Place the mixture in the freezer uncovered for one hour. Drag a fork through the mixture and repeat the process once per hour for 3-4 hours until mixture is crystallized and icy.

CINNAMON SUGAR COOKIES

Yields 72 cookies

Follow instructions for thumbprint cookies. Instead of topping with preserves, sprinkle cookies with sugar and cinnamon immediately after baking, while cookies are still hot.

Raspberry Buttercake Squares dipped in White Chocolate

Serves 16 squares

Crust:

1	box yellow cake mix
¼ cup	butter (½ stick), softened
2	eggs

Filling:

1 cup	frozen raspberries, thawed
4	eggs
16 oz	cream cheese, softened
5 cups	powdered sugar
1 Tbsp	vanilla extract

Preheat oven to 350 degrees.

Crust:

Grease a 15 x 10 glass baking dish with butter. In a large mixing bowl, beat together cake mix, butter and eggs with electric beater until crumbly.

Filling:

Place raspberries in a blender and blend until smooth. Put puree in a medium sauce pan and bring to a boil over medium heat. Continue boiling until reduced in half.

In a mixing bowl combine eggs, cream cheese, powdered sugar and vanilla. Beat until blended. Pour mixture over the crust. Drizzle raspberry puree over the filling in straight lines about 2 inches apart along the length of the pan. Drag a toothpick through the lines in opposite directions every 2 inches. The end result will be a slight rippled look. Bake 30-35 minutes until set and lightly browned on top. Remove from oven and let cool completely. Cut into 2 x 2 inch squares.

½ lb	white chocolate, baking or chips

Place white chocolate into a glass bowl and melt in the microwave on high in 30 seconds increments. Dip each piece of bar dessert halfway into the white chocolate. Place on a baking sheet lined with parchment paper to cool.

Raspberry Rose Vacherin

Serves 4

2 pt	raspberries
12	rose flavored meringue cookies
2 cups	rose water Greek yogurt mousse
1 pt	raspberry sorbet (can be purchase at store)
1	organic edible rose
1	orange, zested and candied, cut into strips
¼ cup	raspberry orange rose reduction

Place one meringue cookie on a plate. Arrange 5 raspberries around the edge of the cookie and fill the center in with about 2 tablespoons of the rose water Greek yogurt mousse. Place a second meringue cookie on top of that and again arrange 5 raspberries around the edge and place 1 small scoop of raspberry sorbet in the middle. Place the third cookie on top of that and dollop 5-6 tablespoons of the yogurt mixture on top of the cookie allowing it to begin to run down the sides of the tower. Garnish the top with rose petals and candied orange peel. Drizzle the plate with a raspberry orange rose reduction.

ROSE WATER MERINGUE COOKIES

Yields 32 cookies

2 lg	egg whites
¾ cup	10 x powdered sugar
1 tsp	concentrated rose water

Preheat oven to 225 degrees. Line a baking pan with parchment paper; do not use wax paper because the meringues will stick to wax paper. In a bowl, beat the egg whites with an electric mixer until they form and hold soft peaks. Once this happens, begin adding the powdered sugar a ¼ cup at a time. Once all the sugar has been added continue to beat the mixture for about 8-10 minutes. The mixture will become very stiff. Fold in the rose water, a little at a time, to the mixture. Drop approximately one tablespoon of meringue onto the prepared baking sheet. Use the back of the spoon the spread out the mixture to the desired shape and size. The meringues will not spread very much. Leave about 2 inches between each of them. Bake the cookies for about 2 hours, until they are completely dry to the touch. If it is humid outside, this can take up to 4 hours. The cookies should be crispy but not brown. Allow to cool for 1-2 minutes and then remove the cookies from the liner paper. Store the cookies in an airtight container for up to one week until ready to use.

ROSE WATER GREEK YOGURT MOUSSE
Yields 2 cups

2 cups	plain Greek yogurt (not low-fat)
1⅛ cups	heavy cream
½ tsp	unflavored gelatin powder
½ cup	10 x powdered sugar
¾ tsp	concentrated rose water

Place a piece of cheesecloth in a sieve or colander that is sitting over a bowl. Put the yogurt in the cheesecloth and allow it to drain for about 30 minutes to one hour. The yogurt will reduce to about one cup. Discard the liquid in the bowl. Place the strained yogurt in the bowl and beat with an electric mixer on low or a whisk until very smooth. Place ⅛ cup of heavy cream in a small saucepan. Sprinkle the gelatin over the cream and let it rest for 5 minutes. Warm the cream and gelatin over low heat and stir until the gelatin is completely dissolved (this may take up to 5 minutes). Remove from heat and allow to cool for about 5 minutes. Pour mixture through a sieve into the strained yogurt. Whisk until incorporated. In another bowl, whip 1 cup of heavy cream with an electric mixer until it is very thick and stiff. Be careful not to over-beat the cream or you will have butter instead of cream. Fold in the powdered sugar and the rose water. Fold the cream mixture into the yogurt mixture about ½ a cup at a time until well incorporated. Refrigerate the mousse for about 4 hours or overnight until completely chilled.

RASPBERRY ORANGE ROSE REDUCTION
Yields ½ cup

½ cup	orange syrup (use left-over syrup from making the candied orange peel)
½ cup	raspberry puree (can be purchased at store)
1 Tbsp	concentrated rose water

Place the orange syrup in a heavy bottom small sauce pan. Bring to a boil over medium heat and add the raspberry puree. Boil for 1 additional minute. Remove from the heat and allow the mixture to cool to room temperature. Add the rose water. Store the reduction in the refrigerator until ready to use.

CANDIED CITRUS PEEL
Yields ½ cup

3 lg	oranges (or lemons, limes or grapefruit)
1 cup	sugar
1½ cups	water
2 cups	granulated sugar

Wash and dry the citrus fruits. Using a vegetable peeler (or paring knife) cut long strips of the citrus peel. Be very careful to not remove any of the white portion of the fruit. This is the pith and it is very bitter. If you accidentally get some of the pith on your citrus strip, turn the strip over and carefully, with your paring knife, remove the pith.

Once you have removed all of the peel of the fruit, cut the long pieces into long thin strips about ¹⁄₁₆-⅛ of an inch in width. Place the citrus strips in a medium, heavy bottom saucepan and cover with cold water. Heat over medium heat until the mixture comes to a boil. Pour the mixture through a strainer. Put the citrus strips back into the saucepan and cover with cold water again. Repeat this process for a total of 3 times. This helps to release the bitter components in the citrus peel. After you have finished that process, place 1 cup of sugar and 1½ cups cold water into the sauce pan. Heat over medium heat, and stir occasionally to make sure that the sugar dissolves. Bring to a boil and boil for approximately 3 minutes. Once the syrup has boiled for 3 minutes, add the citrus strips to the syrup. Reduce the heat and simmer for 10-15 minutes until the strips become translucent. Remove from the syrup and place on a baking sheet covered in wax paper. Spread out and cover with granulated sugar. Allow strips to dry for 1-2 hours or overnight. Store in airtight containers until ready to use.

Red Wine and Cinnamon Pears with Crème Anglaise

Serves 8

8	*Anjou or Bosc pears, peeled, cored, and stem on*
1	*bottle dry red wine, Cabernet or Merlot*
4	*cinnamon sticks*
1 cup	*sugar*
1 cup	*water*

Slice a small amount of the pear off the bottom so that the pears will sit flat when served.

In a large stock pot, place the pears and all of the ingredients. If pears are not completely immersed in the liquid add more water. Bring to a boil over high heat. Reduce heat to low and simmer for 30-45 minutes, until pears are soft but still firm. Remove from heat and let pears cool in the liquid. Refrigerate in the liquid until ready to serve. Serve topped with crème Anglaise.

CREAM ANGLAISE

Yields 1 quart

6	*egg yolks*
½ cup	*sugar*
2 cups	*heavy cream*

Combine the egg yolks and sugar in a medium mixing bowl. Beat the mixture with a hand mixer until the batter is thick and light. Place the cream in a medium sauce pan and heat until scalded or just before boiling. With the mixer running on low, very gradually pour the scalded cream into the egg yolk mixture. Pour the mixture back into the sauce pan and heat it slowly, stirring constantly until thickened enough to coat the back of a wooden spoon. Place the pot in an ice bath and keep stirring until the sauce cools.

Romanoff Sauce

Yields 1 cup

1 cup sour cream
2 Tbsp brown sugar

In a mixing bowl, stir together sour cream and brown sugar. Stir until sugar is dissolved. Refrigerate until ready to use.

Rum Cake

Serves 15

1	*box vanilla cake mix*
1	*4 oz box instant vanilla pudding*
3 Tbsp	*flour*
½ cup	*water*
½ cup	*vegetable oil*
4	*eggs*
½ cup	*dark rum*
⅓ cup	*pecan pieces*

Glaze:

1¼ cup	*butter (1½ sticks)*
1½ cup	*sugar*
½ cup	*water*

Preheat the oven to 350 degrees. Butter and flour a Bundt pan. In a mixing bowl, beat all ingredients (except pecans) with an electric beater until smooth. Place pecan pieces into bottom of Bundt pan and pour cake batter on top of pecans. Bake for 1 hour (or until a toothpick comes out clean). To make the glaze, place butter, sugar and water into a medium, heavy bottomed sauce pan and heat over medium heat until bubbly. When the cake is done, remove from the oven and wait 10 minutes before adding glaze. Pour the glaze over the cake slowly. Use a fork to poke holes in the cake to allow glaze to saturate the cake. Cool the cake in the pan for 30-40 minutes. Once cooled, turned the cake onto a serving platter.

Rustic Pear Gallete
with Amaretto Caramel Sauce
Serves 8

4	boxes refrigerated pie dough
3 lg	Anjou or Bosc pears, peeled, cored, and thinly sliced
½ cup	sugar
¼ cup	white wine
1 tsp	cinnamon
1 Tbsp	flour
1 Tbsp	lemon juice
2 cups	Amaretto Caramel sauce

Preheat oven to 350 degrees. Unroll pie dough cut into 6 inch round pieces. Press the pieces into a 4 inch fluted tart shell pan. Place the tartlet shells on a baking sheet. Place the pear slices, sugar, white wine, cinnamon, flour and lemon juice in a large mixing bowl. Toss to combine. Spoon the apple mixture into fluted 4 inch tart shells. Bake until apples are tender and crust is golden brown, about 30-40 minutes.

Spring Berry Trifle
Serves 10

1 cup	sugar
1 cup	water
4 Tbsp	rum
1 qt	heavy cream
2	frozen pound cakes, thawed, sliced into ½" pieces
4 cups	prepared instant vanilla pudding
2 pt	strawberries, sliced
2 pt	raspberries, washed and dried
2 pt	blueberries, washed and dried
2 pt	blackberries, washed and dried

Place the sugar and water in a medium heavy saucepan. Bring to a boil and continue boiling for 2-3 minutes. Remove from the heat and add the rum. In a separate bowl, whip the heavy cream until stiff peaks are formed. In a large glass serving dish or trifle bowl, place ½ cup sliced strawberries on the bottom of the bowl. Lay slices of pound cake on top of strawberries to cover the bottom of bowl. Drizzle the pound cake with ½ cup sugar rum syrup. Top the cake with 1½ cups vanilla pudding, then top with an assortment of berries. Be sure to place berries all the way to the edge so they can be seen from the outside of the bowl. Top berries with 1 ½ cups whipped cream. Repeat the process once or twice more, until you reach the top of the bowl. The top layer should be whipped cream. Reserve berries for the top of trifle to garnish.

Tartlet Dough
Yields 24 tartlets

¾ cup	butter (1½ sticks), cut into 1 inch pieces
1 cup	flour
1 pinch	salt
1½ Tbsp	sugar
1	egg yolk
2½ Tbsp	cold water

In a food processor, combine butter and flour until crumbly. Be careful not to over beat dough. Add the salt and sugar. Then, add in the egg yolk and water. Process the dough for about 15-20 seconds. Place the dough onto a floured board, and knead the dough by pressing it into a ball. Wrap in plastic wrap and chill in freezer for 20 minutes or in refrigerator for 1 hour. Use a rolling pin and roll chilled dough into ⅛ inch thick round. Place metal tart shells on top of dough and cut a piece around the shell slightly bigger than shell. Press pastry into the tartlet pans and cut off excess with your thumb. If baking, place a second metal tartlet shell pan on top. Bake at 350 degrees for 10-15 minutes, or until golden brown.

NOTE: Some of the following recipes use cooked shells and other raw. Check to see before cooking tartlet shells.

Apple Tartlets
Yields 24 tartlets

6	granny smith apples, peeled, cored and diced small
1 cup	brown sugar
2 Tbsp	flour
1	dash salt
1 tsp	cinnamon
¼ tsp	nutmeg
2 Tbsp	butter, cut into small pieces

Preheat oven to 325 degrees. Mix the apples, brown sugar, flour, salt, cinnamon and nutmeg together. Spoon the mixture into the uncooked tartlet shells. Sprinkle butter on top of apples. Bake for 10-15 minutes until mixture is bubbly. Cool to room temperature.

BASIL BOURBON CARAMEL SAUCE
Serving Size:

1½ cups	granulated sugar
½ cup	water
1 cup	heavy cream
2 Tbsp	Bourbon
¼ cup	minced basil

In a medium sauce pan, whisk sugar and water until sugar is dissolved. Cook over medium heat until the mixture is clear, 2-3 minutes. Increase to medium high heat and brush down the side of the pan with a pastry brush dipped in water (this prevents any sugar from sticking to the side of the pan and forming crystals). Do not stir the mixture. After about 15 minutes you will notice that the bubbles will be getting bigger and slower, just before the caramel begins to turn color. As soon as the caramel turns a medium tan color, remove the pan from the heat. Slowly add the cream. The cream will cause the hot caramel to bubble up. Stir the cream into the caramel with a heat proof spatula. Add the bourbon. Let the caramel sauce cool to room temperature, then refrigerate until ready to use. Right before serving, stir in the basil.

Chocolate Macadamia Nut Tartlet
Yields 24 tartlets

Crust:

⅔ cup	salted macadamia nuts (4 ounces), chopped
¼ cup	flour
¼ cup	sugar
½ cup	butter (1 stick), chilled
2 lg	egg yolks

Filling:

5 oz	semisweet dark chocolate
¾ cup	butter
¼ cup	chocolate shavings, for garnish

Preheat the oven to 350 degrees. In a food processor, pulse together the chopped nuts, flour, sugar, and cold butter until the mixture resembles coarse meal. Add egg yolks, one at a time, and blend the dough until it begins to come together, but still crumbly. Press dough into 1½ inch tartlet shells. Bake the tartlet shells for 10-15 minutes. Cool for 5 minutes. Melt the semi-sweet chocolate and butter together in a double boiler. Stir constantly and do not burn. Remove from the heat and cool slightly. Spoon chocolate into tartlet shells and bake for 20 minutes or until chocolate is set. Cool to room temperature and just before serving garnish with chocolate shavings.

Dark Chocolate Ganache Tartlet

Yields 24 tartlets

5 oz	*semi-sweet dark chocolate (60% cocoa)*
¾ cup	*butter*
1½ cups	*sugar*
½ cup	*flour*
3	*eggs, lightly beaten*
¼ cup	*shaved chocolate*

Melt chocolate and butter together in a double boiler. Stir constantly until chocolate is melted. Remove from heat and cool slightly. Combine the sugar, flour and eggs in a mixing bowl and stir until well blended. Stir into the chocolate mixture. Refrigerate for 3-4 hours. Spoon ganache into 24 1½" baked tartlet shells and top each tart with shaved chocolate.

Key Lime Tartlets

Yields 24 tartlets

Crust:

¾ cup	*butter (1½ sticks), melted*
3 cups	*graham cracker crumbs*

Filling:

8	*egg yolks*
2 cans	*condensed milk*
1 cup	*key lime juice*
½ cup	*heavy cream, whipped*
¼ cup	*lime zest, garnish*

In a mixing bowl, mix together graham cracker crumbs and butter. Blend well. Press crust into 1½ inch tartlet shells. Preheat the oven to 350 degrees. In a medium mixing bowl, beat the

egg yolks with electric mixer until pale yellow. Fold in the condensed milk and lime juice. Do not over beat the mixture. Spoon the filling into prepared tartlet shells. Bake 10 minutes until set. Cool completely. Top with whipped cream and lime zest.

Lemon Curd Tartlets

Yields 24 tartlets

6	*egg yolks, beaten*
1 cup	*sugar*
½ cup	*lemon juice*
½ cup	*butter (1 stick), cut into pieces*
1 Tbsp	*lemon zest*
½ cup	*heavy cream, whipped*
¼ cup	*lemon zest, garnish*

In a heavy bottom sauce pan, beat egg yolks with the sugar and lemon juice. Stir to combine, and cook over medium-low heat, stirring constantly for 10-12 minutes or until the mixture thickens and coats the back of a wooden spoon. Remove from heat and stir until the mixture cools slightly. Whisk in butter, one piece at a time, until fluffy. Stir in the lemon zest. Let cool completely and refrigerate overnight. Spoon the lemon curd mixture into prepared baked tartlet shells. Top with whipped cream and lemon zest.

Raspberry Tartlets

Yields 24 tartlets

¼ cup	*raspberry preserves*
1 pint	*raspberries*

Spoon small amount of raspberry preserve in each shell. Top with a raspberry.

Toasted Coconut Meringue Tartlet

Yields 24 tartlets

½ cup	coconut flakes, sweetened
2	egg yolks
1 cups	coconut milk
¼ cup	buttermilk

Preheat oven to 350 degrees. Place coconut flakes on a baking sheet and place in oven for 5-7 minutes until coconut is lightly browned. Remove from oven and cool to room temperature. In a medium mixing bowl, whisk together the egg yolks, coconut milk and buttermilk. Spoon the mixture into 24 1½" tartlet shells. Bake tarts in the oven for 20-25 minutes until filling is set. Remove from oven. Top with meringue and toasted coconut.

Meringue:

3	egg whites
1 pinch	salt
2 Tbsp	sugar

Preheat the oven to broil.

In a medium mixing bowl, beat the egg whites until soft peaks form. Add salt and sugar. Continue beating for 7-8 minutes or until stiff peaks form and meringue is glossy. Top coconut tartlets with a generous tablespoon of meringue. You may use a piping bag to top tartlets with meringue, if desired. Place in oven and broil for 1-2 minutes until lightly browned (or use a kitchen torch and brown meringue). Sprinkle with toasted coconut and serve immediately.

The Chocoholic

Serves 4

4	chocolate molten cakes, warmed
2 cups	espresso chocolate mousse
1 pt	blackberry cabernet sorbet (store bought)
½ cup	balsamic reduction
1 pt	blackberries, washed and patted dry
½ cup	hazelnuts, toasted
½ cup	chocolate espresso beans (store bought)
4 pcs	white and dark chocolate shards

On a dinner plate, drizzle balsamic reduction from edge to edge. Place warm chocolate lava cake in the center of plate. Spoon the mousse on one side of the cake and one scoop of sorbet on the other side. Garnish plates with toasted hazelnuts, fresh blackberries and chocolate covered espresso beans. Place a chocolate shard into warm molten cake and serve.

ESPRESSO CHOCOLATE MOUSSE

Yields 4 cups

1 cup	whole milk
4 lg	egg yolks
3 Tbsp	sugar
1 Tbsp	instant espresso granules
1 tsp	vanilla extract
7 oz	bittersweet chocolate, chopped
1 cup	heavy cream
1 pinch	salt

Heat whole milk in a small heavy sauce pan until hot. In a medium mixing bowl, beat together yolks, sugar and a pinch of salt until well combined and the mixture is pale yellow. Add the hot milk in a slow stream whisking until well combined. Transfer the mixture into a sauce pan and cook over low heat stirring constantly until custard thickens, about 10 minutes. Stir in the vanilla extract and espresso granules. Melt the chocolate in a glass in microwave on high in 30 second intervals until melted. Remove from the heat and slowly stir chocolate into the custard. Cool to room temperature. Beat the heavy cream in a bowl with an electric mixer until it just holds stiff peaks. Fold the whipped cream into the chocolate mixture. Refrigerate for 4-6 hours until mousse is set.

WARM CHOCOLATE MOLTEN CAKE
Serves 4

6½ oz	bittersweet or semisweet chocolate, chopped
3 Tbsp	butter
4 lg	egg yolks
4 Tbsp	sugar
2 lg	egg whites

Preheat the oven to 425 degrees. Grease four, 6 ounces ceramic ramekins with butter. Dust with flour and shake out the excess. Combine chocolate and butter in the top of a double boiler and set over simmering water. Stir until the chocolate is melted and the mixture is smooth. Remove from heat and cool for 10 minutes. In a large mixing bowl, beat egg yolks and sugar until pale yellow in color, about 2 minutes. Add the egg mixture into the chocolate mixture and stir gently. In a separate clean bowl, beat the egg whites until stiff (be sure to use a dry bowl and beaters). Gently fold the whites into the chocolate mixture. Pour the batter into the prepared ramekins and place the ramekins onto a baking sheet. Bake about 10-15 minutes until the cake has puffed up. The cake will be dry on the outside and soft runny chocolate on the inside. Use a small knife, cut around the sides of the cake in order to loosen the cake from the dish. When ready to serve, turn the ramekins upside down on a plate and allow dark chocolate to run over the plate. May be made ahead and held in refrigerator for up to 2 days. To warm, preheat oven to 450 degrees and warm cakes in ramekins for 10-15 minutes.

BALSAMIC REDUCTION
Yields ¼ cup

½ cup	balsamic vinegar

In a small sauce pan, bring the vinegar to a boil and then reduce to a simmer. Allow the mixture to simmer until the vinegar is reduced by half, about 5 minutes. Remove from heat and cool.

WHITE AND DARK CHOCOLATE SHARDS
Yields 12-16 pieces

6 oz	bittersweet dark chocolate, chopped
4 oz	white chocolate, chopped

Stir dark chocolate in a medium metal bowl set over a sauce pan of simmering water until melted and smooth. Remove the bowl from heat. Place a sheet of parchment paper on a baking sheet. Pour the melted chocolate onto the parchment paper. Work quickly, and use a rubber spatula to spread the chocolate into a thin layer over the paper. Refrigerate for 15 minutes. Stir white chocolate into a small bowl over simmering water until melted. Remove the baking sheet from the refrigerator and drizzle white chocolate over the dark chocolate. Drag a toothpick through to chocolates to make a design. Return to the refrigerator for at least one hour until set. Cut into small pieces.

The Essence of Cream
Serves 4

4	crème caramel
2 cups	caramel sauce
4 sm	crème bruleés
4	buttermilk panna cotta
2 cups	whipped crème fraîche
½ cup	mango pomegranate coulis
4	lace cookies
¼ cup	brown sugar
2	kiwis, peeled and diced
¼ cup	pomegranate seeds
1	orange, peeled and segmented
1 tsp	fleur desel

On a dinner plate, drizzle the caramel sauce in a zig zag pattern from edge to edge. Place one crème bruleé in the ramekin on the plate and invert one crème caramel and place on plate. The caramel will run onto plate. Place one panna cotta on plate. Drizzle additional caramel sauce over the crème caramel and sprinkle lightly with fleur desel. Drizzle the mango pomegranate coulis over the panna cotta and top with a dollop of crème fraîche. Sprinkle the crème bruleé with a pinch of brown sugar and use the hand torch to caramelize. Garnish the plate with diced kiwi, pomegranate seeds and orange segments.

CRÈME CARAMEL WITH CARAMEL SAUCE

Serves 4

Caramel:

1 cup	sugar
½ cup	water

Custard:

½ cup	sugar
3 lg	egg yolks
1 lg	egg
1½ cups	heavy cream
½ cup	whole milk

Preheat the oven to 300 degrees. Lightly butter 4 ceramic ramekins.

Caramel:

Combine the sugar and water in a heavy small sauce pan. Stir over low heat until the sugar is melted. Stop stirring and increase the heat. Bring to a boil and continue cooking until the color turns a deep amber color, about 10 minutes. Brush down the sides of the pan, periodically with a pastry brush dipped in cold water. Once the sugar has turned deep amber, remove from the heat and pour even amounts into the prepared ramekins.

Custard:

Beat the sugar, yolks and egg in a medium bowl until pale in color. Combine the cream and milk in a heavy medium saucepan and heat to just before boiling. Gradually stir the hot cream mixture into the yolk mixture. Pour the custard into the ramekins over the caramel sauce. Fill to ¾ full. Set the ramekins in 13 x 9 inch baking pan. Add enough hot water to the pan to come half way up the sides of the dishes. Cover the baking pan with foil and bake the custards for 55 minutes or until a rounded tip knife comes out clean. Allow the custards to cool uncovered at room temperature for 1 hour, then refrigerate for at least 4 hours. When ready to serve, run the knife around the sides of the ramekin to loosen the custard and then invert onto plates. The caramel sauce will be loose under the custard and will surround the plate.

CRÈME BRULEE

Follow crème brulee recipe, but instead of cooking in a large ceramic dish, pour the mixture into at least 4 small ramekins.

WHIPPED CRÈME FRAÎCHE

Yields 1½ cups

½ cup	heavy cream
½ cup	sour cream
1 tsp	sugar

Beat the heavy cream until stiff. In a separate bowl, stir mix the sugar and sour cream together until the sugar dissolves. Fold in the whipped cream. Refrigerate until ready to serve.

BUTTERMILK PANNA COTTA

Serves 6

1½ tsp	unflavored gelatin
¾ cup	heavy whipping cream
⅓ cup	sugar
1½ cups	buttermilk
1½ tsp	vanilla extract

Pour 1½ tablespoons of water into a small bowl. Sprinkle the gelatin over the water and let stand until the gelatin softens, about 10 minutes. Heat heavy cream and sugar in a heavy bottomed, small sauce pan over medium high heat until sugar dissolves. Heat to just before boiling. Remove from the heat and stir in gelatin until it dissolves. Allow to cool for 5-10 minutes. Add buttermilk and vanilla extract into the mixture. Stir. Pour mixture into at least (6) ½ cup ramekins. Cover and refrigerate until set, at least 4 hours.

MANGO POMEGRANATE COULIS

Yields 1 cup

½ cup	pomegranate juice
½	mango, peeled and seeded
½ cup	sugar
¼ cup	water

In a small sauce pan, boil the pomegranate juice over high heat until reduced to ¼ cup. Puree the fresh mango, sugar and water in a blender and blend until smooth. Pour mixture into the pomegranate reduction and bring to a boil. Continue boiling until reduced by half. Remove pan from the heat and cool completely.

Thumbprint Cookies

Yields 60 cookies

This base recipe is from one of my mother's best friends and I have never found a better recipe.

1 cup	butter (2 sticks)
1 cup	sugar
1	egg
2 tsp	vanilla extract
2 cups	flour
½ tsp	baking soda
½ tsp	cream of tartar
¼ cup	raspberry preserves
¼ cup	strawberry preserves
¼ cup	apricot preserves
¼ cup	blackberry preserves

Preheat the oven to 375 degrees. In a medium mixing bowl, mix together butter and sugar with a spoon. Add the egg and vanilla. In a separate bowl, mix together the flour, baking powder and cream of tartar. Add flour mixture to butter mixture. Take 1 teaspoon of dough and from into a ball. Place dough balls on an ungreased baking sheet. Use a spoon to flatten out the dough and place a small indention in the middle of dough. Cookies should be about 2" apart on the baking sheet. Spoon about ¼ teaspoon of individual preserves into middle of cookies. Bake until golden brown, about 10 minutes. Remove from the oven and cool for 2 minutes on the baking sheet. Move cookies to a rack or plate to cool completely. Store the cookies in an airtight container until ready to use.

Triple Decadence Cake

Serves 12

Cake:

1	box chocolate cake mix
4 cups	chocolate sauce
4 cups	chocolate icing
2 cups	semisweet chocolate chips
1 cup	dark chocolate (60% cocoa), shaved

Make cake according to the box instructions. Do not overcook as cake will be dry. Make a two layered cake. When cake has cooled down, place one of the cake rounds on a serving platter. Spread 1 cup icing over layer. Place second cake round on top and repeat process. Ice sides of cake and refrigerate cake for 1 hour. Gently tap the chocolate chips into the sides of the cake, all the way around. Top the cake with the chocolate shavings. Refrigerate until ready to serve. Serve with warmed chocolate sauce drizzled over the slices.

CHOCOLATE ICING

Yields 4 cups

1¾ cups	heavy cream
¾ cup	butter (1½ sticks)
6 Tbsp	unsweetened cocoa powder
4 Tbsp	powdered sugar
16 oz	semisweet chocolate, chopped

Place the heavy cream, butter, cocoa powder and powdered sugar in medium saucepan. Heat over medium heat until mixture is hot but not boiling. Remove from heat and add chocolate. Stir until chocolate is melted and smooth. Refrigerate frosting for 30-45 minutes until icing is thick but spreadable.

CHOCOLATE SAUCE
Yields 4 cups

¼ cup	butter (½ stick)
¼ cup	unsweetened cocoa powder
½ cup	sugar
1 cup	heavy cream

In a heavy bottomed, medium sauce pan, heat butter and cocoa powder over medium heat. Stir until well combined. Add sugar and cream and stir until well incorporated. Continue heating and stir constantly over medium heat for about 5 minutes.

Upside Down Poached Fruit Cobbler
Serves 12

2	boxes refrigerated pie dough
½ cup	butter (1 stick)
½ cup	sugar
¼ cup	water
2 Tbsp	lemon juice
1 lb	dried apricots
1 lb	dried cherries
1 lb	dried black mission figs

Preheat the oven to 375 degrees. Unroll the pie doughs and press both pieces together. Use a rolling pin and roll them into a large rectangle about 12 x 17 inches. Lay the dough over a 9 x 13 inch glass baking dish and press into dish. Allow excess dough to fall over the edges. Make sure the entire inside of dish is covered in dough, including the sides. In a medium, heavy bottomed skillet, melt butter. Stir in sugar, water and lemon juice. Add all dried fruits and heat over medium heat until the fruits plump. Pour warm fruits onto of dough in baking dish. Pinch excess dough together around top edge of dish. Bake for 20-30 minutes, until dough is golden and the liquid around the fruits is bubbling. Allow to cool slightly. Serve with vanilla ice cream.

White Wine Poached Pears Filled with Mascarpone Mousse
Serves 4

1	bottle white wine
1 cup	water
¾ cup	sugar
1	whole vanilla bean, split
4	firm Bartlett or Anjou pears, peeled, stem intact, and cored from the bottom
1½ cups	mascarpone mousse
1 sm	bunch mint leaves, for garnish

Place the white wine, water, sugar, and vanilla bean into a large sauce pan over medium-high heat. Bring to a boil. Decrease the heat to low and place the pears into the hot liquid. Cover and cook for 30 minutes or until the pears are tender. Remove the pears with a slotted spoon to a platter and refrigerate for 2 hours. Bring the liquid to a boil and continue boiling for 15-20 minutes until reduced in half. Remove the vanilla bean from the syrup and allow the mixture to cool. Refrigerate until ready to serve. When ready to serve, place the mousse in a piping bag. Pipe the mousse with a small tip into the pears core. Drizzle with syrup and garnish with mint leaves.

MASCARPONE MOUSSE
Yields 3 cups

½ cup	sugar
⅓ cup	white wine
3	egg yolks
1 cup	mascarpone cheese
½ cup	heavy cream
½ tsp	vanilla extract

In a medium mixing bowl, whisk sugar, wine and egg yolks. Set bowl over a pot of simmering water. Whisk mixture constantly until it thickens, about 5-6 minutes. Place bowl over a large bowl filled with ice and continue whisking until the custard cools, about 3 minutes. In a separate bowl, stir mascarpone with a rubber spatula to soften. Once the mascarpone is softened, fold in the custard. In a separate bowl, whip the heavy cream until soft peaks form. Add vanilla extract and whip to stiff peaks. Fold into the custard mixture.

MEATS

SALADS